CRUCIAL LIFE SKILLS FOR TEENS

HOW TO BUILD YOUR SELF CONFIDENCE, MANAGE YOUR MONEY, LIVE INDEPENDENTLY, OVERCOME CHALLENGES AND ACHIEVE SUCCESS

FREEDOM PUBLICATIONS

Copyright © 2025 by Freedom Publications. All rights reserved.

The content within this book may not be reproduced, duplicated, or transmitted without direct written permission from the author or the publisher.

Under no circumstances will any blame or legal responsibility be held against the publisher, or author, for any damages, reparation, or monetary loss due to the information contained within this book, either directly or indirectly.

Legal Notice:

This book is copyright protected. It is only for personal use. You cannot amend, distribute, sell, use, quote, or paraphrase any part of the content within this book, without the consent of the author or publisher.

Disclaimer Notice:

Please note the information contained within this document is for educational and entertainment purposes only. All effort has been expended to present accurate, up-to-date, reliable, and complete information. No warranties of any kind are declared or implied. Readers acknowledge that the author is not engaged in the rendering of legal, financial, medical, or professional advice. The content within this book has been derived from various sources. Please consult a licensed professional before attempting any techniques outlined in this book.

By reading this document, the reader agrees that under no circumstances is the author responsible for any losses, direct or indirect, that are incurred as a result of the use of the information contained within this document, including, but not limited to, errors, omissions, or inaccuracies.

CONTENTS

Introduction   5

1. Building Financial Literacy and Independence   9
2. Emotional Intelligence and Resilience   23
3. Practical Life Skills for Everyday Success   37
4. Digital Literacy and Online Safety   51
5. Communication and Relationship Building   67
6. Time Management and Goal Setting   81
7. Self-Discovery and Personal Growth   95
8. Preparing for the Future: Career Planning and Beyond   109

Conclusion   121
References   125
About the Publisher   131

INTRODUCTION

Hi, once upon a time I was a teenager and when I was a teenager, I found myself standing at a crossroads, unsure of which path to take. Like many of my peers, I struggled with self-doubt, fear of failure, and the overwhelming pressure to succeed in a rapidly changing world. It was during this time that I discovered the power of developing crucial life skills. This discovery not only transformed my own journey but also ignited a passion for empowering others.

In today's fast-paced, ever-evolving society, teenagers face many challenges that extend far beyond academic achievements. From navigating complex social dynamics to making critical decisions about their future, the demands placed upon young minds can be daunting. That's where this book comes in, a comprehensive guide designed to equip teenagers with the essential tools they need to build confidence, resilience and independence.

Within these pages, we'll explore a wide range of topics that are vital to personal growth and success. From developing emotional intelligence and effective communication skills to cultivating a growth mindset and practicing self-care, we'll dive into the nitty-gritty of what it takes to thrive in the face of adversity. We'll also tackle practical matters such as financial literacy, time management and digital wellness, ensuring that you have a well-rounded tool-kit to navigate the modern world.

This book is for you, the curious teenager eager to unlock your full potential, the concerned parent seeking guidance on how to support your child's development, or the passionate educator looking to foster a generation of resilient and independent thinkers. Whether you're just starting your journey or well on your way, this book will meet you where you are and provide you with the insights and strategies you need to take your skills to the next level.

What sets this book apart is its engaging, hands-on approach. We'll explore real-life examples, participate in thought-provoking exercises and engage in meaningful reflections that will help you internalize the lessons and apply them to your own life. This isn't just another self-help book that you'll read and forget; it's a dynamic, interactive experience that will challenge you to step outside your comfort zone and embrace personal growth.

Now, I know what you might be thinking: "Life skills? Isn't that just common sense?" While it's true that some of these concepts may seem intuitive, the reality is that many teenagers struggle to put them into practice. We live in a society that often prioritizes academic achievements over emotional intelligence and as a result, many young people find themselves ill-equipped to handle the challenges of adulthood. By addressing these misconceptions head-on and providing a structured framework for skill development, this book aims to bridge that gap and empower you to take control of your own growth.

As we embark on this journey together, I encourage you to approach each chapter with an open mind and a willingness to learn. You'll find that the book is organized into distinct sections, each focusing on a specific set of skills or themes. Feel free to dive in wherever you feel most drawn, or work through the chapters sequentially the choice is yours. What matters most is that you engage with the material, reflect on your own experiences and take action to implement what you've learned.

My own journey has taught me that developing crucial life skills is a lifelong process, one that requires patience, persistence and a healthy dose of self-compassion. As your guide and companion on this path, I promise to support you every step of the way, offering insights, encouragement and a touch of humor to keep things light. Together, we'll celebrate your successes, learn from your setbacks, and cultivate the resilience and adaptability you need to thrive in an ever-changing world.

So, are you ready to embark on this transformative journey to build the confidence, resilience and independence you need to overcome challenges and achieve your wildest dreams? If so, turn the page and let's get started. Your future self will thank you.

1

BUILDING FINANCIAL LITERACY AND INDEPENDENCE

Have you ever found yourself at the checkout counter, heart pounding as you swipe your card, praying it doesn't get declined? Or maybe you've experienced the dreaded "low balance" alert just when you were about to splurge on that much-needed pair of shoes? If you have, you're not alone. We've all been there, navigating the sometimes treacherous waters of personal finance, often without a life vest. But fear not! This chapter is your trusty guide to financial literacy and independence, helping you sail smoothly into the realm of budgeting, saving and spending wisely.

Understanding and managing your money is not just about avoiding embarrassing moments at the cash register. It's about empowering you to make informed decisions, gaining control over your financial future, and eventually achieving your goals, whether it's buying your first car, saving for college, or planning that dream vacation. Mastering these skills early on gives you the confidence to tackle life's challenges head-on, without the added stress of financial uncertainty.

1.1 BUDGETING BASICS: CRAFTING A PERSONAL BUDGET YOU CAN STICK TO

Let's kick things off with budgeting, a word that might sound about as exciting as watching paint dry, but trust me, it's your best friend in the financial world. Budgeting is essentially the art of telling your money where to go, instead of wondering where it went. It's about taking control of your finances by planning your spending and saving habits, ensuring you have enough for the things that matter most. For teens, budgeting is crucial because it lays the foundation for financial stability and independence as you transition into adulthood.

Creating a realistic budget starts with identifying your income sources. This might include your allowance, part-time job earnings, or even birthday money. Once you've got a clear picture of what's coming in, it's time to categorize your expenses. Think of expenses as either fixed i.e. those that are consistent each month, like your phone bill, or variable, such as the occasional coffee run or an impromptu movie night. Tracking these spending habits helps you identify patterns and areas where you might cut back. With this information in hand, you can create a simple budget template that outlines your income, expenses and savings goals.

Now, let's talk about some common budgeting pitfalls and how to dodge them. Overspending on non-essentials is a trap we've all fallen into at some point. That killer sale might seem irresistible until you realize you're left with pennies for the rest of the month. Then there's failing to account for irregular expenses like birthday gifts or seasonal clothing purchases, which can throw your budget off balance. And let's not forget those sneaky small daily expenses, yes, that morning latte adds up. Being mindful of these pitfalls and planning for them in your budget can save you from financial headaches down the road.

Thankfully, we live in a digital age where budgeting tools and apps are just a tap away, ready to make the process smoother. Apps like *Mint, PocketGuard* and *YNAB (You Need A Budget)* are fantastic resources for tech-savvy teens. They help track your spending, set budget limits and even alert you when you're approaching those limits, ensuring you stay on track. These tools simplify managing your finances and make the process more engaging, so you won't find yourself in a financial pickle when payday finally arrives.

Budgeting might seem daunting at first, but with a little practice and patience, it becomes second nature. Think of it as a skill you're honing, like playing an instrument or mastering a new sport. The more you practice, the better you become at making strategic financial decisions that align with your goals. Plus, as you gain confidence in managing your money, you'll find that budgeting opens up a world of possibilities, allowing you to save for the things you love while still covering your essentials. So grab a notebook, download an app and start crafting a budget that works for you. Your future self will thank you for it.

1.2 SAVING STRATEGIES: BUILDING YOUR FIRST EMERGENCY FUND

Picture this: you're cruising down the road, feeling like the king or queen of the universe, when suddenly your car starts making a noise that sounds suspiciously like an angry robot. Or imagine you wake up one morning to find that your beloved smartphone has decided to take an impromptu swim in the kitchen sink. These scenarios, while seemingly outlandish, are precisely why an *emergency fund* is your best ally. An emergency fund is a stash of money set aside for unforeseen expenses, think medical emergencies, car repairs, or urgent travel needs. It's your financial buffer, preventing you from spiraling into debt or resorting to drastic measures like borrowing from parents or racking up credit card bills.

Now, let's chat about setting realistic savings goals. Start by assessing your *monthly savings capacity*. This means figuring out how much money you can comfortably set aside each month after covering your basic expenses. It doesn't have to be a large amount; consistency is key. Once you've identified your savings capacity, it's time to establish short-term and long-term goals. Short-term goals might include saving for concert tickets or a new gadget, while long-term goals focus on building that emergency fund to a comfortable level, say $500 or $1,000, as a solid starting point.

To kickstart your saving habits, consider a few actionable strategies. Automating savings transfers can be a game-changer. Set up an *automatic transfer* from your checking account to your savings account each month, this way, you won't even miss the money. Another approach is using savings jars or envelopes. Label each jar or envelope with a specific savings goal and drop in spare change or small bills whenever possible. For a fun twist, challenge yourself with "No-Spend Weekends," where you spend nothing on non-essential items for a couple of days. These habits might sound simple, but they lay the foundation for consistent saving behavior.

Let's not forget the magic of *compound interest*. It's like a secret ally working behind the scenes to grow your savings over time. Compound interest means you earn interest not just on your initial savings but also on the interest that accumulates over time. Imagine planting a money tree that keeps growing and growing. The earlier you start saving, the more time your money has to grow exponentially. To illustrate, if you start saving $50 a month at 16, with an annual interest rate of 5%, you could have over $10,000 by the time you're 30, proof that small amounts can lead to big outcomes.

Incorporating these saving strategies into your daily life can transform your financial outlook. It might seem daunting initially, but the sense of security and peace of mind you'll gain is worth every penny saved. Remember, you don't need a windfall to start building your emergency fund. Small, consistent efforts add up over time, ensuring you're prepared for whatever life throws your way. Whether it's an unexpected car breakdown or a surprise medical bill, having an emergency fund means you can face those challenges head-on without breaking a sweat.

1.3 CREDIT CARDS AND LOANS: UNDERSTANDING INTEREST AND AVOIDING DEBT

Imagine walking into a store, picking up whatever you fancy and walking out without handing over a dime. Sounds like a dream, right? Well, that's the illusion credit cards can create, but beware, this financial tool can morph into a nightmare if not handled with care. A credit card is like a financial lifeline that allows you to borrow money for purchases, promising to repay it at a later date. Meanwhile, loans, which come in various forms, provide larger sums for significant expenses like education or a car, often with a structured repayment plan. The key difference between them lies in their purpose and scope. Loans can be secured, meaning they're backed by collateral like a house or a car, or unsecured, where there's no collateral but often heftier interest rates. Understanding the nature of these financial instruments is crucial because they can either help you build a sound financial future or lead you into a debt trap.

Interest is the cost of borrowing money and it's where things can get sticky. With credit cards and loans, you're not just repaying what you borrowed, you're also paying extra for the privilege of using someone else's money. This extra cost is calculated as a percentage of the borrowed amount, known as the interest rate. Higher interest rates mean more money out of your pocket over time, which is why it's crucial to manage credit wisely. Misusing credit cards, such as carrying a high balance with only minimal payments, can lead to compounding interest charges, quickly turning a small purchase into a large debt. Imagine buying a $100 item on credit with a 20% interest rate and only paying the minimum each month; that item could end up costing you significantly more. The longer you take to pay it off, the more interest piles up, leaving you in a debt spiral that's hard to escape.

To steer clear of such debt traps, there are a few golden rules to follow. First, always aim to pay more than the minimum balance on your credit card each month. This approach not only reduces the interest you'll pay but also helps you clear your debt faster. Secondly, resist the temptation of impulse purchases on credit. It might be easier said than done, but sticking to planned spending can save you from endless bills. Lastly, understand your credit limits and stick to them. Maxing out your credit card not only racks up debt but can also negatively affect your *credit score*, a three-digit number reflecting your creditworthiness.

Your credit score is more than just a number; it's your financial reputation. Lenders use it to decide whether to lend you money and at what interest rates. Factors influencing it include payment history, amounts owed and the length of your credit history. Consistently paying bills on time and keeping credit card balances low are surefire ways to maintain a healthy score. Remember, a good credit score opens doors to better loan terms and lower interest rates, saving you money in the long run.

Case Study: The Credit Card Conundrum

Let's consider a typical scenario. You're a college student who just got your first credit card. Excited by the newfound freedom, you start using it for everything from textbooks to takeout. A few months in, you realize you've maxed out your limit. The minimum payment seems manageable, but the interest starts accumulating. Soon, your monthly bill is more than you anticipated, leaving you stressed and scrambling to make ends meet. By following the strategies outlined above, paying more than the minimum, avoiding unnecessary purchases and monitoring your credit score, you can turn this situation around and regain control over your finances.

Financial literacy empowers you to make informed decisions and avoid common pitfalls, setting you up for a secure and prosperous future.

1.4 INVESTING 101: SIMPLE STEPS TO START GROWING YOUR WEALTH

Picture this: you're sitting on a park bench, minding your own business, when suddenly, a friendly squirrel drops an acorn in your lap. At first, you might think, "Great, a snack!" But then you remember that squirrels are onto something. They don't eat every acorn they find. Instead, they bury some for the future. That's what investing is all about, planting seeds today so that you can enjoy the fruits tomorrow. Investing means putting your money into financial vehicles with the hope of growing it over time. Unlike saving, where you stash cash away safely, investing involves taking calculated risks to potentially earn more. While saving is akin to securing a nest egg, investing is about growing that egg into a golden goose.

To start, let's explore a few common investment vehicles that even beginners can navigate. *Stocks* represent ownership in a company and when you invest in them, you're buying a piece of that company. If the company does well, your stock's value may increase, potentially earning you a profit. *Bonds*, on the other hand, are loans you give to entities like governments or corporations. They promise to pay you back with interest, typically offering a more stable, albeit lower, return compared to stocks. *Mutual funds* pool money from various investors to buy a diversified portfolio of stocks and bonds, while *Exchange-Traded Funds* (ETFs) are similar but trade on stock exchanges like individual stocks. Each offers different levels of risk and reward, and understanding these can help you make informed decisions.

Now, you might be wondering how to start investing when your budget is as tight as your favorite pair of skinny jeans. Fear not! You can begin with small amounts by exploring *fractional shares*, which allow you to purchase *partial shares* of expensive stocks. This way, you can invest in high-value companies without needing a hefty bankroll. Another option is *robo-advisors*, digital platforms that create and manage an investment portfolio for you based on your financial goals and risk tolerance. They provide a hands-off approach, perfect for those who are just getting their feet wet in the investing pool.

One of the cornerstones of investing is *diversification*, which means spreading your investments across various assets to reduce risk. Imagine a fruit basket filled with only apples. If the apple market takes a hit, you're in trouble. But if your basket has apples, oranges and bananas, you're better protected. Similarly, diversifying your investment portfolio ensures that if one asset underperforms, others can help cushion the blow. Understanding your risk tolerance, how much risk you can comfortably take on, plays a crucial role in deciding how to diversify. Some folks are thrill-seekers, ready to ride the ups and downs of the stock market, while others prefer the safety net of bonds or low-risk funds.

Interactive Element: Build Your Investment Portfolio

Create a mock portfolio using a free online investment simulator such as 'eToro' or 'thinkorswim'. Select a mix of stocks, bonds and ETFs that align with your risk tolerance and financial goals. Track their performance over a month, noting any changes in value and how they affect your overall portfolio. Reflect on what you learn about diversification and risk management.

Investing isn't just for the wealthy elite or Wall Street wizards. It's a powerful tool that can help anyone grow their wealth over time, even if you start small. By planting the seeds of investment early, you're setting yourself up for a bountiful future. With a bit of knowledge, a dash of patience and a willingness to learn, you can navigate the world of investing with confidence and watch your money work for you.

1.5 SMART SHOPPING: HOW TO MAKE YOUR MONEY GO FURTHER

Shopping can be an exhilarating experience, akin to a treasure hunt where the goal is not just to find what you need but to snag it at the best possible price. However, smart shopping is more than just filling your cart with sale items, it's about making informed decisions to maximize the value of every dollar spent. Start by comparing prices before buying. This doesn't mean hopping from store to store like a caffeinated rabbit. Instead, harness the power of the internet. Price comparison websites and apps can do this legwork, allowing you to see where your desired item is cheapest. Recognizing marketing tactics is also crucial. Retailers are skilled at making products look irresistible, often using bright displays, limited-time offers, and even charming music to entice you. Being aware of these strategies helps you stay focused on what you really need, not what the store wants you to buy.

Saving money while shopping doesn't mean you have to sacrifice quality. For instance, using coupons and discounts is a tried-and-true method. Keep an eye out for digital coupons or subscribe to store newsletters for exclusive deals. Timing your purchases for sales can also lead to significant savings. Just like how certain fruits are best in season, some products are cheaper at specific times of the year. For example, electronics often drop in price around Black Friday or during back-to-school sales. Buying in bulk is another excellent strategy, especially for non-perishable items like toothpaste or toilet paper. By purchasing larger quantities, you often pay less per unit, stretching your dollars further without compromising on quality.

Impulse buying can wreak havoc on your wallet, often leading to buyer's remorse and unnecessary clutter. To keep this at bay, create a shopping list and stick to it. This simple act helps you focus on what you truly need, preventing those pesky impulse purchases. Another effective tactic is the 24-hour rule for non-essential items. If you find yourself tempted by something that isn't on your list, wait a day. This cooling-off period often reveals whether the item is a true necessity or just a passing fancy. By practicing these strategies, you can take control of your spending habits, ensuring that your hard-earned money goes to items that genuinely add value to your life.

When it comes to shopping, the age-old debate of quality versus quantity often arises. Investing in high-quality items, although they may cost more upfront, can save you money in the long run. Consider the concept of cost-per-use calculations. For instance, a pair of well-made shoes that last five years has a lower cost per wear than a cheaper pair that falls apart after a season. By prioritizing durability, you can avoid the cycle of frequent replacements, ultimately leading to long-term savings. It's about finding that sweet spot where value meets longevity. High-quality products tend to perform better, last longer and provide greater satisfaction over time.

So, the next time you're out shopping, remember to keep these strategies in mind. Whether you're navigating the aisles of a bustling mall or scrolling through an online store, these tips will help you make wise purchases that maximize your financial resources.

1.6 FINANCIAL GOAL SETTING: TURNING DREAMS INTO ACHIEVABLE PLANS

Imagine waking up one morning with a vision, a life filled with opportunities, adventures and financial security. Sounds dreamy, right? That's the beauty of setting financial goals. They transform abstract ideas into tangible plans, motivating you to take charge of your financial decisions and steering you toward the life you imagine. A financial goal is essentially a target you set for managing your money, whether it's saving for a new laptop, planning a summer trip with friends, or even thinking about your future education. Goal setting in personal finance is like having a GPS for your money; it keeps you on track and prevents you from getting lost in the endless options that life throws your way.

To effectively set financial goals, the *SMART framework* comes to the rescue. This stands for Specific, Measurable, Achievable, Relevant and Time-bound. Specificity is key, it's the difference between saying "I want to save money" and "I want to save $500 for a new bike by June." By defining exactly what you're aiming for, you create a clear roadmap to follow. Measurability allows you to track your progress, like checking off each mile on a road trip. Achievability ensures your goals are within your reach; it's about stretching yourself without setting up for failure. Your goals should also be relevant, aligning with your personal values and priorities. Lastly, setting a time frame gives your goals urgency and helps you maintain focus.

Tracking and adjusting your goals is just as important as setting them. Think of it as tuning a guitar; you need to make adjustments to keep everything harmonious. Financial planners or journals are great tools for this. You can jot down your goals, note your progress and make tweaks as needed. Regular financial reviews say, once a month, help you assess what's working and what isn't. Maybe you need to save a bit more this month or adjust your timeline due to unexpected expenses. Being flexible and open to change ensures your goals remain relevant and achievable.

Accountability plays a significant role in keeping you on track. Sharing your goals with someone you trust, be it a friend, family member, or mentor, provides support and motivation. This person can cheer you on, offer advice, or even give you a gentle nudge if you start to stray. Joining financial goal groups or clubs can also be beneficial. These communities offer a sense of camaraderie and shared purpose, making the whole process more engaging and less daunting. It's like having a workout buddy at the gym, you're more likely to stick to your routine when someone else is counting on you.

As you embark on this exciting adventure of financial goal setting, remember that it's not just about reaching the destination. The skills you develop along the way, discipline, planning, accountability, are invaluable assets that will serve you well in all areas of life. Whether you're saving for something small or dreaming big, each step you take brings you closer to making those dreams a reality. So go ahead, set those goals, and watch as your financial landscape transforms before your eyes. With determination and a sprinkle of creativity, there's nothing you can't achieve.

2

EMOTIONAL INTELLIGENCE AND RESILIENCE

Picture yourself standing in front of a massive maze. You can't see the exit and every path looks the same. Now, imagine you have a magic map that guides you through. This map represents emotional intelligence, a skill that helps navigate the labyrinth of life's emotions. Understanding and managing your emotions is like having a superpower that allows you to make better decisions, build stronger relationships and generally not freak out when things go sideways. It's not just about knowing whether you're feeling happy or sad; it's about recognizing the intricate web of emotions we experience daily and using this knowledge to enhance your life.

2.1 EMOTIONAL AWARENESS: KNOW YOUR FEELINGS

Emotional awareness is crucial because it serves as the backbone of *emotional intelligence*. When you can accurately identify and name your feelings, you're better equipped to make decisions that align with your values and goals. Think about it: If you're aware that you're feeling anxious about an exam, you can address that anxiety by studying more or seeking help rather than just feeling overwhelmed. This awareness allows you to respond thoughtfully instead of reacting impulsively. Moreover, emotional awareness lays the foundation for empathy, enabling you to understand and connect with others on a deeper level. It's like having a secret decoder ring that helps you interpret not only your emotions but also those of others, fostering more meaningful interactions.

So, how can you become an emotion-naming ninja? One effective technique is to create an *emotion wheel*. This visual tool helps you identify and categorize a wide range of emotions, from the basic, like joy and anger, to the more nuanced, like frustration or contentment. By regularly exploring this wheel, you become more adept at pinpointing exactly what you're feeling and why. Another helpful practice is *journaling your emotional experiences*. Writing about your day and how certain events made you feel allows you to reflect and gain insights into your emotional patterns. Over time, you'll notice trends and triggers, empowering you to take proactive steps toward emotional well-being.

The interplay between thoughts and emotions is like a dance, each influencing the other in a delicate waltz. *Cognitive-behavioral techniques* can help you understand this relationship better. By examining your thought patterns and how they affect your emotions, you can learn to reframe negative thoughts into more positive ones. For instance, if you catch yourself thinking, "I'll never pass this test," you can challenge that belief with evidence of past successes or a plan to improve your study habits. Thought-emotion journaling exercises can also be beneficial. By documenting your thoughts alongside your emotions, you develop a clearer picture of how they intertwine, giving you greater control over both.

Emotions play a pivotal role in interpersonal relationships, shaping how we communicate and connect with one another. Understanding your own emotions can significantly improve your interactions with others. For example, if you recognize that you're feeling irritable, you might take a moment to breathe and collect yourself before responding to a friend's comment. This pause can prevent unnecessary conflict and promote more harmonious communication. Emotional awareness also enhances your ability to resolve conflicts effectively. By recognizing the emotions at play in a disagreement, you can address the underlying issues with empathy and understanding, facilitating a more constructive dialogue.

Interactive Element: Emotion Wheel Exercise

Create your own emotion wheel with different segments for primary emotions like happiness, sadness, and anger. Further divide these into more specific feelings, such as elation, frustration, or contentment. Reflect on your day and place your emotions on the wheel, noting any patterns or triggers. This exercise will help you develop a more nuanced understanding of your emotional landscape.

By cultivating emotional intelligence, you unlock a wealth of benefits that extend far beyond your internal world. You enhance your decision-making abilities, deepen your empathy for others and foster more fulfilling relationships, setting the stage for personal and social success. Embrace the magic map of emotional intelligence and watch as it transforms your path through the maze of life.

2.2 STRESS MANAGEMENT TECHNIQUES: FINDING YOUR CALM IN CHAOS

Ever felt like you're juggling flaming swords while riding a unicycle on a tightrope? Welcome to *stress*, your body's reaction to feeling overwhelmed. When stressed, your body kicks into its fight-or-flight mode, ready to battle a saber-toothed tiger or, more likely, tackle a mountain of homework. Your heart races, breath quickens, and muscles tense, a response that's helpful when facing actual danger but less so when your biggest threat is a pop quiz. Over time, chronic stress can wreak havoc on your system, leading to headaches, sleep issues and a constant craving for snacks you know aren't great for you.

Luckily, managing stress doesn't require a magic wand or a one-way ticket to a deserted island. Breathing exercises are a simple yet effective tool. Imagine you're blowing up a balloon, slowly inhaling through your nose, filling your lungs, and then letting it out through your mouth. This sends a signal to your brain to chill out, reducing stress and anxiety. Progressive muscle relaxation is another handy trick. Starting from your toes, tense each muscle group for a few seconds, then release, working your way up. You'll feel the tension melt away, like a popsicle on a hot summer day. Guided imagery, where you picture yourself in a tranquil setting, a beach, a forest, or a world where math homework doesn't exist, can also transport you to a place of calm.

Physical activity is a natural stress-buster, turning that bundle of nerves into a bundle of energy. Pilates, with its stretches and deep breathing, acts like a reset button for your mind and body. Whether you're a seasoned exerciser or can barely touch your toes, exercises' calming effects can help you completely relax and zone out. Cardiovascular exercises, like running or cycling, release endorphins, those feel-good chemicals that lift your mood and relieve stress. Plus, they give you a legitimate excuse to wear those fancy running shoes you bought on sale.

Creating a personal stress management plan is like crafting your own superhero toolkit. Start by identifying what triggers your stress. Is it that looming deadline, the thought of doing your homework, taking an exam, being around other people in a social setting, or just the daily hustle and bustle? Once you know your triggers, implement daily practices to keep stress at bay. Maybe it's a five-minute morning meditation, a brisk walk during lunch, or even a nightly dance party in your room. The key is to find what works for you and make it a regular part of your routine. Stress might be as inevitable as taxes, but learning to manage it means you can face life's challenges with a clear mind and a steady heart.

2.3 BUILDING RESILIENCE: BOUNCING BACK FROM SETBACKS

Imagine *resilience* as your personal superhero cape, draped around your shoulders, ready to help you face whatever life throws your way. Resilience is the ability to bounce back from setbacks, adapt to change, and keep going in the face of adversity. It's the mental toughness that helps you get back up after a fall, brush off the dust, and say, "Is that all you've got?" Resilient individuals often share certain characteristics: they possess a positive outlook, are flexible in their thinking, and maintain a strong sense of purpose. They're like those inflatable clown toys that pop back up no matter how many times they're knocked down. Through resilience, you can transform challenges into stepping stones rather than stumbling blocks, making it a key predictor of success and personal growth.

Developing a resilient mindset doesn't require a trip to a superhero boot camp. It's about learning how to view negative events through a different lens. Positive reframing is one such strategy.

Rather than fixating on failure, try to see it as a learning opportunity. Did you flunk a test? Sure, it stings, but what can you learn from it? Maybe you need different study techniques or more time to prepare. By setting and achieving small goals, you can build confidence and resilience over time. Think of it like climbing a mountain. You don't leap to the top in one giant bound. Instead, you take it step by step, each small victory fueling the next until you've reached the summit.

Enter the concept of a *growth mindset*, a powerful ally in fostering resilience. Unlike a fixed mindset, which believes abilities are static, a growth mindset thrives on the idea that skills and intelligence can be developed through dedication and hard work. It's the belief that, with effort, you can improve. To nurture a growth mindset, focus on the process rather than the outcome. Praise effort, not just results. If you struggle in a particular subject, remind yourself that it's an opportunity to grow rather than a testament to your limitations. Embrace challenges as a chance to learn, and view setbacks as temporary hurdles rather than permanent roadblocks.

History is replete with examples of resilience. Consider the story of Thomas Edison, who famously failed thousands of times before perfecting the light bulb. When asked about his repeated failures, he reportedly said, "I have not failed. I've just found 10,000 ways that won't work." His relentless perseverance eventually led to one of the most significant inventions in history, the light bulb. Once perfected by his colleague Lewis Latimer, resulted in a light bulb not only illuminating our homes but also the path of resilience. Or think of Helen Keller, who, despite being deaf and blind, became an author, activist and lecturer, proving that resilience knows no bounds. She once said, "Optimism is the faith that leads to achievement." These stories serve as powerful reminders that resilience isn't about avoiding failure but rather embracing it as part of the journey toward growth and success.

To cultivate resilience, start by recognizing your own strengths and resources. Reflect on past experiences where you've overcome difficulties and draw upon those lessons as you face new challenges. Surround yourself with supportive individuals who uplift you and encourage your efforts. Practice self-care and maintain a balanced perspective, focusing on what you can control and letting go of what you cannot. Remember, resilience isn't just about bouncing back; it's about growing stronger with each bounce, turning life's challenges into opportunities for personal development. With resilience as your cape, you can face the world with confidence, ready to tackle whatever comes your way.

2.4 MINDFULNESS PRACTICES: STAYING PRESENT AND FOCUSED

Imagine your mind as a bustling train station, with thoughts whizzing by like high-speed trains. At times, it can feel overwhelming chaotic, even as you attempt to catch one thought before the next arrives. That's where *mindfulness* comes in, a gentle conductor guiding each train to the right track, bringing order and calm to the station. Mindfulness is the practice of focusing on the present moment without judgment. It's about observing your thoughts and feelings from a distance, acknowledging them without getting tangled up in them. This practice can improve focus, reduce stress and enhance emotional well-being and it's backed by science. Research shows that mindfulness can help lower stress levels, improve attention, and even boost your immune system. It's like a master key, unlocking doors to a healthier mind and body.

Incorporating mindfulness into your daily routine doesn't require a yoga mat or an incense stick, simple exercises can do wonders. Take the *body scan meditation*, for example. This involves mentally scanning your body from head to toe, tuning into sensations without trying to change them. It's like a mental inventory, helping you become more aware of where you might be holding tension. Then there's *mindful breathing*, which is as simple as it sounds. Focus on each breath, noticing the rise and fall of your chest. If your mind wanders, gently bring it back to your breath. Practicing *gratitude journaling* is another powerful tool. Spend a few minutes each day writing down things you're grateful for. It shifts your focus from what's wrong to what's right, fostering a more positive mindset.

Mindfulness also plays a significant role in emotional regulation. By practicing mindful observation, you can reduce emotional reactivity. When an emotion arises, notice it without judgment. Observe how it feels in your body what thoughts accompany it, and let it pass without clinging to it. This technique helps you respond to emotions rather than react impulsively. It's like being the calm eye of a storm, where you can see the chaos around you but remain centered. Through regular practice, mindfulness can help you manage and regulate your emotions more effectively, improving your overall emotional balance.

Integrating mindfulness into everyday activities can make it more accessible and less of a chore. Mindful eating, for instance, involves savoring each bite noticing the flavors, textures, and aromas. It transforms a routine meal into a delightful experience, helping you appreciate food and prevent overeating. Then there's mindful walking, where you pay attention to each step, the sensation of your feet touching the ground and the rhythm of your breath. It's like pressing a pause button on the hustle and bustle, allowing you to enjoy the journey rather than rush to the destination.

Interactive Element: Mindful Breathing Exercise

Try this: find a quiet place to sit comfortably. Close your eyes and take a deep breath in through your nose, hold it for a moment, and then exhale slowly through your mouth. Count to four as you inhale, hold for four and exhale for four. Repeat this cycle for a few minutes, focusing solely on your breath. Notice how your body feels as you breathe and let any distracting thoughts drift away like clouds in the sky.

By weaving mindfulness into your daily routine, you cultivate a sense of calm and clarity that extends beyond the practice itself. It's like planting seeds of tranquility, nurturing them with attention and care and watching them grow into a flourishing garden of peace and presence. Whether you're studying for exams, dealing with a difficult situation, or simply going about your day, mindfulness offers a way to stay grounded and focused amidst the noise.

2.5 HEALTHY COPING MECHANISMS: ALTERNATIVES TO NEGATIVE BEHAVIORS

Picture this: you're at a school dance and the DJ suddenly cuts the music. Awkward, right? That's how it feels when life throws stress your way without warning. Developing healthy coping mechanisms is like having a playlist ready to keep the beat going. These strategies not only help you manage stress in the moment but also set you up for emotional well-being in the long haul. When you rely on positive coping techniques, you build resilience and reduce the risk of turning to unhealthy behaviors that can spiral out of control, like binge-watching TV shows all night or indulging in junk food until your stomach protests.

So, what are some positive ways to handle the curveballs life throws at you? Art and creative expression are fantastic outlets. Whether it's doodling in the margins of your notebook or painting a masterpiece, *engaging in creative activities* allows you to channel emotions constructively. It's like having a conversation with your soul, minus the awkward pauses. *Journaling* is another powerful tool. By putting pen to paper, you can release pent-up feelings and gain clarity on challenging situations. Think of it as a brain dump, a way to clear mental clutter and make sense of what's happening in your life. Engaging in hobbies and interests, from playing a sport to baking cookies, provides a sense of accomplishment and joy, drawing your focus away from stress and onto something you love.

Recognizing and *replacing negative coping behaviors* is key to maintaining a healthy balance. Start by identifying triggers for those not-so-great habits. Maybe you reach for a bag of chips whenever you're overwhelmed, or perhaps you lash out when you're feeling anxious. Once you've pinpointed these triggers, create a plan for behavioral change. Instead of raiding the snack drawer, try taking a walk or calling a friend. Gradually replace unhelpful habits with positive ones and soon you'll find yourself naturally gravitating toward healthier choices. It's like swapping out a screechy violin for a soothing cello. It's the same instrument family, but with a much better vibe.

Never underestimate the power of *social support* when it comes to coping. Having a network of friends, family, or professionals to lean on can make all the difference. Talking to someone you trust about what you're going through can provide comfort and perspective. Whether it's a heart-to-heart with your best friend or a candid chat with your favorite teacher, sharing your burdens lightens the load. In some cases, seeking professional help, like *counseling or therapy*, is a valuable step. A counselor or therapist can guide you through tough times, offering tools and insights tailored to your unique situation. Building a support network is like assembling a team of superheroes, each person brings their own strengths and together, they help you tackle life's challenges with confidence.

Healthy coping mechanisms are about more than just surviving tough times; they're about thriving despite them. By embracing positive strategies, you cultivate emotional resilience and equip yourself to face whatever challenges come your way. Remember, life might throw a few curveballs, but with the right coping tools in your back pocket, you're ready to knock them out of the park.

2.6 THE ART OF SELF-COMPASSION: BEING KIND TO YOURSELF

Imagine treating yourself with the same kindness and understanding that you offer a friend who's having a tough day. That's *self-compassion* in action. It's about acknowledging your struggles without judgment and offering yourself comfort and care. While *self-esteem* hinges on how you perceive your worth relative to others, self-compassion centers on being kind to yourself, especially during failures or mistakes. It's a gentle reminder that it's okay to be human. Unlike self-esteem, which fluctuates based on external validation, self-compassion provides a steady foundation for emotional health, helping you weather life's storms with grace and understanding.

Practicing self-compassion doesn't mean letting yourself off the hook for everything. It's about using kind and forgiving language when you talk to yourself. Instead of berating yourself for a mistake, try saying, "It's okay, everyone slips up sometimes." This shift in language can make a world of difference. Engaging in self-compassion meditations can also foster a nurturing mindset. These meditations often involve visualizing a compassionate presence, offering you warmth and acceptance. Writing a self-compassion letter is another powerful exercise. In this letter, write to yourself as if you were writing to a dear friend, acknowledging your feelings and offering support. These practices help cultivate a kinder, more forgiving attitude toward yourself, which can transform your inner dialogue.

The impact of self-compassion on mental health is profound. Research shows that self-compassion can reduce anxiety, depression and stress, acting as a buffer against the pressures of daily life. In one study, participants who practiced self-compassion reported greater emotional resilience and lower levels of stress over time. Real-life case studies further illustrate its benefits. Take, for example, a student who used self-compassion techniques to cope with academic setbacks. By reframing her self-critical thoughts and treating herself with kindness, she was able to bounce back from failures with renewed motivation and confidence. These examples underscore how self-compassion can serve as a powerful tool for emotional well-being.

To develop a self-compassionate mindset, start by challenging self-critical thoughts. When you catch yourself spiraling into negativity, pause and question the validity of those thoughts. Are they based on facts, or are they distortions of reality? Replace them with more balanced, compassionate perspectives. Celebrating personal achievements, no matter how small, is also crucial. Take a moment to acknowledge your successes, whether it's acing a test or simply getting out of bed on a tough day. These celebrations create a positive feedback loop, reinforcing the belief that you are worthy of love and kindness, even from yourself.

Incorporating self-compassion into your life is like planting seeds of kindness that bloom into a garden of resilience and strength. It might feel strange at first, after all, many of us are more accustomed to self-criticism than self-kindness. But with practice, you can cultivate a self-compassionate mindset that supports you through life's ups and downs. Remember, being kind to yourself isn't about being selfish; it's about recognizing that you deserve the same compassion and care that you readily offer others. As you embrace self-compassion, you pave the way for greater emotional health and a more fulfilling life.

3

PRACTICAL LIFE SKILLS FOR EVERYDAY SUCCESS

3.1 BASIC COOKERY AND CULINARY ADVICE: MASTERCHEF 101

Imagine stepping into a *kitchen* for the first time, like an explorer entering a new world filled with mysterious gadgets and tantalizing aromas. The kitchen might seem intimidating, but it holds the key to independence, health and even financial savvy. *Cooking* is more than just a survival skill, it's a passport to freedom. Picture this, not only do you get to whip up delicious meals that impress your friends and family, but you also save money and eat healthier. When you cook at home, you're the boss of your plate, choosing what goes into your meals and controlling the portions. Plus, there's the undeniable satisfaction of saying, "Oh, this? I made it myself."

The benefits of cooking at home extend beyond the kitchen. It's like having a secret weapon for better health and a thicker wallet. By preparing your meals, you avoid the hidden sugars and fats lurking in takeout and fast food. This means fewer chances of having to squeeze into those jeans after a weekend of indulgence. Financially, home-cooked meals are a game-changer. You can whip up a hearty dinner for the price of a latte and those savings add up over time. Think about it, the more you cook, the more you save and suddenly, that new gadget or those concert tickets don't seem so out of reach.

Before you don the chef's hat, let's talk about tools and ingredients. A few essential kitchen utensils will make your culinary adventures a breeze. Start with a good *knife* set, sharp enough to cut through a tomato without squishing it, but not so sharp that it turns into a horror movie prop. A sturdy *cutting board, pots and pans* are your trusty sidekicks, along with a *mixing bowl* and a *spatula* for when you need to channel your inner Gordon Ramsay. As for ingredients, stock up on pantry staples like *rice, pasta* and *canned goods*. They're versatile and can be the base for countless meals, saving you from the dreaded "there's nothing to eat" moment.

Now, let's dive into some easy recipes that are as kind to your budget as they are to your taste buds.

Spaghetti aglio e olio is a minimalist's dream, just pasta, garlic, olive oil, and a sprinkle of red pepper flakes. It's quick, satisfying, and makes you feel like you've just stepped into an Italian café. For a veggie-packed option, a simple stir-fry with rice is perfect. Toss in whatever vegetables you have, add some soy sauce and voilà, a colorful, nutritious meal.

And when breakfast feels like a chore, whip up an *omelet* (Omelette) with your favorite fillings. Whether it's cheese, spinach, or last night's leftovers, an omelet is a blank canvas for your culinary creativity.

Meal planning and prep are your allies in the battle against time and food waste. Creating a weekly meal plan helps you organize your shopping list and ensures you use up what you buy. It's like having a roadmap for the week, saving you from those last-minute "what's for dinner?" panics. Batch cooking is another lifesaver. Spend a day cooking a few dishes that can be frozen and reheated when you're in a pinch. Imagine having a homemade meal ready in the time it takes to scroll through your social media feed. Not only does this save time, but it also reduces food waste, making both your wallet and the environment happy.

Interactive Element: Pantry Checklist

Create a checklist of pantry essentials to keep on hand. Check your kitchen and add any missing items to your shopping list. These staples will be the backbone of your meals, helping you whip up something delicious even when the fridge looks empty.

Cooking might seem daunting at first, but with practice, it becomes a rewarding, creative pursuit. You'll soon find yourself experimenting with flavors and techniques, turning everyday meals into culinary masterpieces. So grab your apron, and let the kitchen adventures begin!

3.2 BASIC CAR MAINTENANCE: WHAT EVERY TEEN DRIVER SHOULD KNOW

Imagine that you're cruising down the highway, windows down, music blasting, feeling like the king or queen of the road. Suddenly, a warning light flashes on your dashboard and your heart sinks. Panic sets in as you wonder what it means and how much it will cost to fix. Sound familiar? This is why basic car maintenance can be ever so useful. Regular maintenance isn't just about avoiding those dreaded mechanic bills, it's about ensuring your ride is safe, reliable and ready for any adventure. By keeping up with routine checks, you can catch minor issues before they become major headaches, saving you both time and money. Plus, there's a certain pride that comes with knowing you're taking care of your own set of wheels.

Let's talk about some must-know maintenance checks that will keep your car in top shape:

First up, *oil levels and changes*. Think of oil as your car's lifeblood, keeping the engine parts running smoothly. It's crucial to check the oil regularly and change it as recommended in your car's manual. To check the oil, make sure the engine is cool, locate the dipstick, pull it out, wipe it clean, reinsert it, and then pull it out again to see the level. If it's low, top it up with the correct type of oil for your vehicle. Changing the oil involves draining the old oil, replacing the oil filter and adding fresh oil, like giving your car a fresh start.

Next, *tire pressure and tread inspection*. Properly inflated tires ensure better fuel efficiency and handling. Use a tire pressure gauge to check the pressure found in your car's manual or inside the driver's doorjamb. As for tread, use the penny test: insert a penny into the tread with Lincoln's head down. If you can see all of his head, it's time for new tires.

And don't forget the *windshield wiper blades*; they're your first line of defense against rainstorms. Replace them every six months to ensure clear visibility.

Now, let's tackle some common car issues and how to troubleshoot them. Ever come out to a car that just won't start? It might be a *dead battery*. To jump-start a car, you'll need *jumper cables* and a second vehicle. Connect the positive (red) cable to the positive terminals of both batteries, then the negative (black) cable to the negative terminal of the working battery and a metal part of the dead car. Start the working car, let it run for a few minutes and then try starting yours. As for those pesky dashboard warning lights, they're like your car's way of saying, "Hey, something needs attention!" Your car's manual will help you decode these alerts, from low tire pressure to engine issues. Ignoring them is like ignoring a text from your best friend, which is never a good idea.

Keeping a *maintenance log* is like having a diary for your car. Every time you perform a check or get a service done, jot down the date, mileage and what was done. This not only helps you keep track of when the next service is due, but it also comes in handy if you ever decide to sell your car. Future buyers love to see a well-maintained vehicle and a detailed log proves you've been taking care of business. Create a schedule based on your car's manual, noting when to check oil, rotate tires, or replace filters. It's a bit like planning dentist appointments, it is annoying but necessary for long-term health.

Taking charge of your car's maintenance means you're ready for whatever the road throws your way. You might not become a fully-fledged mechanic overnight, but with these basics down, you'll navigate car ownership with confidence. So grab your toolkit, check that dipstick and keep your ride running smoothly.

3.3 HOME REPAIRS 101: TACKLING SIMPLE FIXES WITH CONFIDENCE

Imagine the satisfaction of fixing a *leaky faucet* or *unclogging a sink* all on your own. It's like being the hero in your own home repair saga; a cape is not required.

DIY home repairs aren't just about saving money (though your wallet will definitely thank you), they're about empowerment, a chance to flex those self-sufficiency muscles and gain the confidence that comes with solving everyday problems, plus, DIY projects can be surprisingly fun, transforming a tedious chore into a mini-adventure. Imagine the cost savings each repair you tackle means more cash in your pocket for things you actually enjoy, like pizza or concert tickets. You get to say goodbye to those hefty service fees that seem to multiply faster than you can say "plumber."

Let's tackle some common household repairs that anyone can master.

Unclogging a sink or drain, for instance, is a task that can go from minor annoyance to major headache if left unchecked. Start by removing any visible debris from the drain. If that doesn't work, a *plunger* can be your best friend. Create a seal around the drain, give it a few firm pumps and watch as the clog releases like a stubborn cork. For more persistent blockages, a chemical-free solution of baking soda and vinegar might do the trick. Then there's the infamous *leaky faucet*, that relentless drip-drip-drip that keeps you up at night. The culprit is usually a worn-out washer. Turn off the water supply, disassemble the faucet, replace the washer, and reassemble. Voila! Peaceful silence. Patching small holes in walls is another common challenge. Whether from a wayward doorknob or an enthusiastic darts game, holes happen. All you need is some spackle or other filler, a putty knife and a little sandpaper. Apply the spackle, smooth it out, let it dry and sand until even. It's like erasing a mistake, satisfying and almost magical.

To tackle these repairs, you'll need a basic *toolkit*. Think of it as your DIY survival kit, complete with a *hammer* and *nails* for those unexpected picture-hanging emergencies. A *screwdriver* set is crucial; you'll use it more times than you can count, whether assembling furniture or fixing that wobbly chair. An *adjustable wrench* is a versatile hero, perfect for plumbing jobs and other tasks that require a *strong grip*. These tools are like trusty sidekicks, always ready to help you save the day. And remember, investing in quality tools now saves you headaches later. You'll thank yourself when that stubborn screw finally gives way with ease.

Remember to ensure your safety at all times when carrying out any DIY repairs. Using protective gear like *eye goggles* and *gloves* is non-negotiable when working with tools. You don't want your DIY adventure to end with a trip to the emergency room. It's also vital to know your limits.

Some repairs, though, are, of course, best left to professionals, especially when dealing with electricity or gas. If a project feels like it's spiraling out of control, there's no shame in calling in reinforcements. It's better to be safe than sorry and less expensive than fixing a DIY disaster. Remember, even the most seasoned DIY veterans consult the pros for the really tricky stuff.

Every repair you tackle is a step toward greater independence and confidence. It's a bit like gaining a new superpower, one that turns you into the master of your own domain. With each fix, you'll feel a sense of accomplishment and pride, knowing you've taken charge and made your space a little better. So roll up those sleeves, grab your toolkit and let the repairs begin. Your newfound skills might even impress your friends and family, just be prepared for them to call you when their sink clogs.

3.4 PERSONAL HYGIENE: ESTABLISHING A SELF-CARE ROUTINE

Picture yourself stepping into a room full of people, feeling confident and ready to take on the world. Your secret weapon? Stellar personal hygiene. It's not just about avoiding funky odors or bad breath, though those are definitely bonuses. *Good hygiene* is a cornerstone of *physical health* and *self-esteem*. By maintaining a clean and healthy body, you reduce the risk of infections and illnesses while boosting your confidence. There's something empowering about knowing you've got your hygiene game on point, like having an invisible shield of freshness. Plus, let's face it, nobody wants to be the person people avoid standing next to in a crowded elevator.

Establishing a daily hygiene routine is like setting a solid foundation for your day. Start with a refreshing shower to wash away the night's sleep and prepare you for whatever comes your way. A shower is not just about getting clean, it's also invigorating, setting the tone for the day. Follow it up with good oral hygiene, brushing and flossing your teeth to keep your smile bright and your breath minty fresh. Regular skincare is also key, especially if you're dealing with the joys of teenage skin. A simple regimen of cleansing, moisturizing and applying sunscreen can work wonders. And don't forget hair care. Whether you're rocking a buzz cut or long locks, regular washing and grooming keeps your hair healthy and looking its best.

Nutrition and exercise might not be the first things that come to mind when you think about hygiene, but they're crucial players in the game. Staying hydrated is like giving your skin a refreshing drink; it helps maintain elasticity and a healthy glow. Drinking water throughout the day also aids in flushing out toxins that could otherwise cause breakouts or dullness. Meanwhile, exercise plays a dual role, keeping you fit and reducing stress while also helping to regulate body odor. Sweating it out at the gym (or wherever you prefer) releases endorphins, the feel-good hormones and keeps your internal systems in check, which in turn supports your overall hygiene.

Life isn't always predictable, and sometimes maintaining hygiene in specific situations can feel like navigating an obstacle course. For instance, traveling can throw your routine for a loop. Packing travel-sized essentials like toothpaste, deodorant and face wipes can help you stay fresh on the go, even if you're hopping between time zones or spending hours on a cramped bus. Similarly, managing hygiene during sports activities requires a bit of planning. A quick rinse after a game, fresh clothes and a reliable deodorant can save you from feeling (or smelling) like you've been marinating in a gym bag all day.

Interactive Element: Hygiene Travel Kit Checklist

Create a checklist for a hygiene travel kit. Include items like mini shampoo, conditioner, toothpaste, toothbrush, deodorant, face wipes and hand sanitizer. Check your kit before trips to make sure you're always prepared.

Hygiene isn't just about routine; it's about feeling good in your skin and presenting your best self to the world. By prioritizing personal care, you not only improve your health but also radiate confidence and positivity. Whether you're gearing up for a big day at school, a night out with friends, or simply lounging at home, good hygiene is your ally.

3.5 ORGANIZING YOUR SPACE: CREATING A FUNCTIONAL AND INSPIRING ENVIRONMENT

Think of your living space as the ultimate reflection of who you are. It's your sanctuary, your launchpad and sometimes, your idea factory. An organized environment isn't just about aesthetics, it's a powerhouse for productivity and peace of mind. Imagine walking into your room and instantly finding what you need without the frantic search that makes you feel like you're in a game of hide and seek with your socks. A tidy space helps clear mental clutter, letting you focus on what truly matters. When everything has its place, you can say goodbye to the stress of lost items and hello to a smoother, more efficient day.

The secret to a well-organized space lies in effective decluttering and smart storage solutions. Begin by sorting and categorizing your belongings. This doesn't mean tossing everything that doesn't spark joy like a certain tidying guru might suggest (though it's not a bad start).

Separate items into categories: *keep, donate, or toss*. It's like giving your room a digital detox but for real life. With fewer distractions, you create more mental space to breathe and think. Once sorted, use storage solutions like bins, shelves, and boxes to maximize space. Stackable bins are like Tetris for your closet, they make every inch count without toppling over like a bad Jenga move.

Personalizing your space is just as important as organizing it. Your environment should reflect your personality and interests, offering inspiration at every glance. Whether it's a gallery wall of your favorite art, a cozy reading nook, or even a quirky collection of knick-knacks, let your space tell your story. Integrate personal decor elements that make you smile. Maybe it's a string of fairy lights that turn your room into a magical escape or a vibrant rug that adds a pop of color. Creating a study or work-friendly area is key, too. A dedicated desk or table, free of distractions, helps you buckle down and focus. A comfortable chair and good lighting can transform a study session from a chore into a productive endeavor.

Maintaining this oasis of order requires a few reliable habits. Regular cleaning schedules can keep chaos at bay. Dedicate a few minutes each day to tidying up, and you'll avoid the dreaded weekend cleaning marathon. Implement a "one in, one out" policy to prevent clutter from creeping back in. For every new item you bring into your space, let go of something you no longer need. It's like a balance beam for your belongings, keeping everything in check. You'll find that a little discipline goes a long way in preserving the harmony of your environment.

When you organize your space, you're not just aligning your physical world. You're setting the stage for creativity, relaxation and productivity. An orderly environment empowers you to focus on what really matters, freeing up time and mental energy for the things you love. Whether preparing for a big test, hosting friends, or simply unwinding with a good book, a well-organized space can make all the difference. So, roll up your sleeves, channel your inner Marie Kondo and transform your living space into the ultimate haven where you can thrive.

3.6 NAVIGATING PUBLIC TRANSPORTATION: GETTING AROUND SAFELY AND EFFICIENTLY

Public transportation might seem like a maze of buses, trains and timetables, but once you get the hang of it, it's like having a golden ticket to freedom. Imagine cruising through a city without the hassle of parking or the panic of running out of gas. Public transit systems are more than just a way to get from point A to point B;

they're a lifeline for many, offering access to work, school and all the fun places in between. Plus, using public transportation is a win-win for both the planet and your wallet. Fewer cars mean less pollution and those saved pennies from skipping the Uber can add up to a nice treat, say, a weekend getaway or a new gadget.

Planning your route on public transit can feel like solving a puzzle, but with a little practice, you'll become a pro. Start by familiarizing yourself with transit maps and schedules. These are the keys to understanding the routes and timing of buses and trains. They're often color-coded, like a giant coloring book for grown-ups, showing you the way with lines and stops. Transit apps are game-changers, providing real-time updates and helping you navigate with ease. Some even offer step-by-step directions so you know exactly when to hop on or off. With these tools, you can plan your journey down to the minute, avoiding that awkward moment of standing at the wrong platform while your ride zooms by.

Safety is your trusty sidekick when using public transportation. Being aware of your surroundings is crucial, especially in bustling stations or crowded trains. Keep an eye on your belongings and hold onto your bag in a way that makes pickpockets think twice. It's like a dance of awareness, staying alert without being paranoid.

When waiting for a bus or train, stand back from the edge of the platform and stay in well-lit areas if traveling at night. Trust your instincts. If something doesn't feel right, it probably isn't. Share your location with a friend or family member, letting them know your estimated arrival time. It's like having a digital buddy system, providing peace of mind for you and your loved ones.

Public transport comes with its quirks, but with a little know-how, you can handle them like a seasoned commuter. Missed connections are a common hiccup, but not the end of the world. If you miss your train, check the schedule for the next one or look for alternative routes. Sometimes, a short walk to another stop can save you precious time. Crowded buses or trains can feel like a sardine can, but they don't have to ruin your day. Find a spot to stand where you feel comfortable and don't be afraid to politely ask someone to move if they're taking up more than their fair share of space. Remember, everyone is just trying to get somewhere and a little kindness goes a long way.

Public transportation opens doors to new adventures, offering a sustainable and affordable way to explore. Once you get the hang of it, you'll find yourself navigating like a local, discovering new places and experiences along the way. So next time you're contemplating how to get across town, consider hopping on a bus or train. It's an opportunity to sit back, relax and let someone else do the driving. Plus, who knows? You might just discover a new favorite coffee shop or park along your route.

As you master these practical life skills, you're not only becoming more independent but also preparing yourself for whatever life throws your way. Whether it's cooking a meal, fixing a leaky pipe, or catching the right bus, you're building a foundation for success. In the next chapter, we'll dive into digital literacy and online safety, equipping you with the skills to navigate the digital world with confidence.

4

DIGITAL LITERACY AND ONLINE SAFETY

4.1 UNDERSTANDING YOUR DIGITAL FOOTPRINT

Imagine wandering through a bustling marketplace, each stall offering glimpses of your life, photos, comments, likes and even that embarrassing video of you attempting the latest dance craze. Unbeknownst to many, this is your digital footprint, a collection of all your online activities etched into the virtual sands. Unlike your charmingly awkward dance moves, your digital footprint isn't something you can easily erase. It's a testament to your online presence, impacting everything from your privacy to your reputation. In a world where digital interactions mirror face-to-face encounters, understanding your digital footprint is akin to knowing which selfie angle works best for you, which is crucial if you want to put your best foot forward.

Every click, post and purchase adds to your digital footprint, creating a permanent record accessible to anyone with a decent Wi-Fi connection. Social media posts, online purchases, and even seemingly innocuous comments contribute to this digital legacy. Imagine your digital footprint as footprints in the sand. Each action leaves a mark that can be traced back, sometimes long after the tide has washed over. The implications of these digital traces are far-reaching. A single post today could influence a college admission officer's decision tomorrow or sway a prospective employer's opinion years down the line. In fact, a 2017 survey showed that 11% of college admissions were denied due to social media content, while another 7% had offers rescinded for the same reason.

Managing your digital footprint is like tidying up your bedroom, i.e., essential for maintaining a sense of order and privacy. Regularly reviewing and cleaning up your social media profiles can prevent those dreaded Saturday night selfies from haunting you forever. Consider adjusting privacy settings to control who can view your posts and personal information. Many platforms offer privacy checkup tools, allowing you to manage your data and control third-party access. Be mindful of sharing personal details, much like you wouldn't broadcast your home address to a room full of strangers. By curating your online presence, you protect yourself from unwanted scrutiny and potential misuse of your information.

Your digital footprint can have a significant impact on future opportunities, influencing everything from college admissions to job prospects. Admissions officers and employers often evaluate candidates' online personas to gauge their character and values. Sharing positive content, such as community involvement or personal achievements, can leave a favorable impression. Highlighting your strengths and goals on social media can showcase your potential beyond academic excellence, aligning with the values institutions and companies seek. Remember, your digital presence should reflect the best version of yourself, steering clear of content that might raise eyebrows or send the wrong message.

To keep tabs on your digital footprint, consider utilizing tools designed to monitor and control your online information. *Google Alerts* can notify you whenever your name pops up on the web, helping you stay informed about your digital presence. Online reputation management services can assist in managing your personal brand, ensuring that your online image aligns with your aspirations. These tools offer insight into how you present yourself online, empowering you to make informed decisions about what to share and what to keep private.

Interactive Element: Digital Footprint Checkup

Set aside time for a digital footprint checkup. Search your name online and review the results. Note any content that might raise concerns or misrepresent you. Adjust privacy settings and remove or update content as needed. Reflect on how you can create a more positive online presence moving forward.

Recognizing the importance of your digital footprint is the first step toward taking control of your online identity. By staying aware and proactive, you can ensure that your digital presence reflects the person you are and aspire to be, leaving a positive impression wherever the digital winds may take you.

4.2 SOCIAL MEDIA SAVVY: NAVIGATING PLATFORMS SAFELY

Imagine social media as a bustling digital city, where each platform is a different neighborhood with its own vibe and set of rules. Instagram is like an artsy district, full of stunning visuals and curated aesthetics. You can share photos, videos, and stories that vanish after 24 hours, making it a playground for creativity. Snapchat, on the other hand, feels like a trendy, fast-paced area where everything happens in the blink of an eye. Messages disappear after being viewed, and with features like Snap Maps, you can share your location with friends (or not, if you prefer to keep your whereabouts a mystery). Then there's TikTok, the vibrant, ever-changing hub where short videos reign supreme. From hilarious skits to jaw-dropping dances, it's all about quick, engaging content. Each platform offers public and private profiles, where you control who gets to peek into your digital life. Public profiles are like open doors, welcoming everyone in, while private ones are more like VIP access only, meaning only those you approve can see your content.

While social media can feel like a big digital party, it's important to protect yourself and your privacy. Avoid oversharing personal information like your home address, birth date, or financial details. Remember, if you wouldn't shout it out in a crowded room, it's best not to post it online. Social media platforms also provide tools for reporting inappropriate content, so don't hesitate to use them. If something makes you uncomfortable or crosses a line, flag it. It's like being a good neighbor, keeping the community safe and respectful. Managing your friend and follower lists is crucial, too. Curate your social circles thoughtfully, just as you would in real life. Quality over quantity, having a smaller group of trusted connections is often better than having a large number of casual acquaintances.

The double-edged sword of social media lies in its impact on *mental health*. On one hand, it offers a platform for connection, creativity, and self-expression. On the other, it can lead to anxiety, depression, and a sense of inadequacy. A quick scroll through

Instagram can feel like a highlight reel of everyone else's perfect life, leaving you with a case of FOMO (fear of missing out) and self-doubt. Studies have shown a correlation between heavy social media use and mental health challenges, highlighting the importance of finding balance. Mixing online interactions with offline activities is, therefore key. Spend time with friends in person, pursue hobbies that don't involve screens, and enjoy the world beyond the digital realm. It's like a balanced diet for your mind and the variety keeps it healthy and happy.

As you navigate the digital landscape, critical thinking becomes your trusty compass. Social media is a melting pot of information, but not all of it is reliable. Fake news and misinformation can spread like wildfire, leading to confusion and mistrust. Approach content with a discerning eye. Check sources, question sensational headlines, and consider the motives behind the information. Influencers and sponsored content are another layer to consider. While influencers can be entertaining and inspiring, remember that they often have partnerships with brands. It's important to differentiate genuine recommendations from paid promotions. Think of yourself as a digital detective, piecing together the truth amidst the noise.

Understanding each platform's features, protecting your privacy, and maintaining your mental well-being are all part of the experience. By staying informed and thoughtful, you can enjoy the benefits of social media while keeping yourself safe and grounded.

4.3 CYBERBULLYING: RECOGNIZING AND RESPONDING EFFECTIVELY

Imagine scrolling through your phone, expecting a cute cat video to brighten your day, but instead, you're hit with a torrent of nasty comments. That's *cyberbullying*, harassment, exclusion, or impersonation in the digital realm. Unlike traditional bullying, which might happen in the schoolyard, cyberbullying follows you home. It invades your space through screens, making it feel inescapable. This digital menace can take many forms, from sending harmful messages to spreading rumors or even pretending to be someone else to damage reputations. It's like a virtual punch to the gut, leaving emotional bruises that can sting just as much as physical ones.

Recognizing the signs of cyberbullying is crucial to tackling it head-on. Behavioral changes are often the first clue. If you notice someone withdrawing from social activities, their mood constantly shifting, or their phone suddenly becoming a source of stress rather than joy, cyberbullying might be at play. Keep an eye on online interactions for negative patterns. Are there recurring names popping up in the comments, or is there a suspicious lack of communication from someone who used to be active? These could be red flags. It's like being a detective, piecing together clues to uncover a hidden issue.

Once you've identified cyberbullying, knowing how to respond can make all the difference. Start by documenting evidence. Screenshots can be your best friends here, capturing exactly what's happening before it disappears. This documentation is crucial when reporting incidents to social media platforms or authorities. Blocking and reporting bullies on the platform is a direct way to cut off their access. Most social media sites have built-in mechanisms for this, making it easy to take action. Don't hesitate to reach out for support from trusted adults, whether it's a parent, teacher, or counselor. It might be difficult for you, but they can provide guidance and help you navigate the situation. It's like assembling a superhero team of people who are on your side and have your best interest at heart, each member bringing strengths to combat the cyberbully.

Creating a supportive online community starts with promoting kindness and empathy. Imagine a digital space where everyone uplifts each other, where positivity drowns out negativity. Engaging in digital citizenship activities can help foster such an environment. This involves encouraging respectful communication, celebrating diversity, and standing up against bullying when you see it. The ripple effect of these actions can be powerful, creating a culture that discourages bullying and supports those who might be targeted. It's about building a virtual neighborhood where everyone feels safe and valued.

Visual Element: Cyberbullying Awareness Infographic

Consider creating or finding an infographic (visual image) that highlights key statistics about cyberbullying, its impacts and steps for prevention. This visual aid can help communicate the seriousness of the issue and offer practical advice at a glance.

Cyberbullying is a challenge that requires vigilance and empathy to overcome. By understanding its forms, recognizing its signs and knowing how to respond, you can protect yourself and others from its harmful effects. Building a positive, supportive online community is not just an aspiration but a responsibility we all share. By working together, we can make the digital world a better place for everyone.

4.4 PRIVACY SETTINGS AND PASSWORDS: PROTECTING YOUR PERSONAL INFORMATION

Imagine your personal information as a treasure chest filled with your secrets, passwords and maybe a few embarrassing selfies you'd rather not share with the world. Protecting this treasure is crucial, especially in an age where data breaches and identity theft are as common as sneezing in allergy season. Weak security measures, like using "password123" or "123456," are like leaving your treasure chest unlocked, practically inviting troublemakers to waltz in and help themselves. When hackers breach your data, they can cause chaos, from emptying your bank account to impersonating you online. So, safeguarding your personal information isn't just smart; it's necessary.

To start fortifying your digital fortress, dive into the world of *privacy settings* on your devices and accounts. Each social media platform offers unique privacy controls, allowing you to decide who can see your posts and personal details. Start by navigating to your account settings, usually found under a menu icon, often resembling three dots or lines. Here, you can adjust who sees your content, ensuring that only trusted friends or family have access. Don't forget about app permissions on your smartphone. Many apps request access to your camera, microphone, or contacts without needing them. Head to your phone's settings, find the app section, and review which permissions you've granted. This step is crucial in preventing apps from peeking into areas they shouldn't.

Creating *strong passwords* is like crafting a secret handshake that only you know. Avoid common pitfalls like using your pet's name or your birthday. Instead, opt for a combination of letters, numbers and symbols. For example, transform "ilovepizza" into "1L0v3P!zza"—a simple tweak that makes it significantly harder to crack. Password managers are fantastic tools for keeping track of these complex combinations. They store your passwords securely and can even generate new, strong passwords for you. Multifactor authentication adds an extra layer of security, requiring a second verification step, like a text message code, before accessing your account. Think of it as a digital bouncer, ensuring only you get past the velvet rope.

Regular security audits might sound like something out of a spy movie, but they're just routine checkups for your digital life. Periodically reviewing your privacy settings and security measures helps keep your accounts secure.

Start with a checklist: update passwords, review privacy settings, and remove any old or unused accounts. Consider setting a reminder every few months to conduct these audits. It's like a digital spring cleaning, ensuring your treasure chest remains locked tight. By actively managing your online security, you not only protect your personal information but also gain peace of mind, knowing you're a step ahead of potential threats.

4.5 EVALUATING ONLINE INFORMATION: SEPARATING FACT FROM FICTION

Imagine you're at a carnival with dazzling lights and mesmerizing music, each booth promising something fantastical. The internet is much like this: a vibrant wonderland of information. But not every booth holds the truth. Some are filled with misinformation, ready to lead you astray. Recognizing this is crucial because misinformation can spread faster than a juicy rumor in high school. Think about the chaos that ensues when false news is shared, creating panic, confusion, and sometimes even endangering lives. Confirmation bias, our tendency to favor information that aligns with our beliefs, only adds fuel to this fire. It's like wearing blinders, seeing only what we want to see, which makes it even harder to distinguish fact from fiction.

To become an informed digital detective, start by scrutinizing the author's credentials. Is the writer a credible expert in their field, or just another keyboard warrior with opinions masquerading as facts? Cross-referencing the information with reputable sources is also key. If you read something shocking, check if it's reported by established outlets like the BBC or National Geographic. It's akin to fact-checking a friend's wild story by asking other friends who were there. This cross-verification helps ensure you're not falling for a cleverly disguised hoax. Another pro tip is to look for peer-reviewed sources or those backed by research, as they usually undergo rigorous scrutiny before publication.

Algorithms, those invisible hands shaping your online experience, play a significant role in the information you see. They decide which posts appear on your feed, often based on your past interactions. This can create an echo chamber where you only encounter views similar to your own. It's like living in a bubble where everyone agrees with you, limiting exposure to diverse perspectives. To burst this bubble, diversify your information sources. Follow a variety of news outlets, engage with different viewpoints and challenge your own biases. Think of it like sampling dishes from around the world instead of sticking to your usual burger and fries diet.

When you feel the urge to share that jaw-dropping headline, pause and verify. Sharing misinformation has a ripple effect, spreading falsehoods far and wide. Before you hit share, ask yourself: Is this true? Can I trust the source? If in doubt, hold back. Promoting digital literacy among your peers can also help combat misinformation. Encourage discussions about source credibility and the importance of fact-checking. It's like being the responsible friend who reminds everyone not to text and drive.

By cultivating critical thinking skills, you equip yourself to navigate the digital landscape with confidence. You become the savvy explorer who knows which paths to take, which to avoid and how to enjoy the carnival without getting swindled by the snake oil salesman. As you sharpen these skills, you'll find yourself not only better informed but also a beacon of truth in the ever-expanding online wilderness.

4.6 BALANCING SCREEN TIME: FINDING A HEALTHY DIGITAL DIET

Picture this: you've spent hours scrolling through memes, updating your avatar's wardrobe and watching endless cat videos. Suddenly, you look up and realize the sun has set and your eyes feel like they've been glued to screens forever. Welcome to *digital overload*, a modern-day phenomenon that leaves you feeling frazzled and drained. The signs are all too familiar: headaches, strained eyes and a general feeling that you've morphed into a zombie in your own life. But fear not, for digital wellness is here to restore balance. Maintaining a healthy relationship with screens allows you to enjoy the benefits of technology while also embracing the richness of life offline. It's like having your cake and eating it too, but without the sugar crash.

Finding this balance involves a *digital detox*, a conscious effort to unplug and recharge. Just like a spa day for your mind, a digital detox involves stepping away from screens and immersing yourself in the tangible world around you. The benefits are undeniable. Clarity returns, creativity sparks and relationships strengthen when you shift your focus from the virtual to the physical. A digital detox can be as simple as a weekend without screens or a daily hour dedicated to being tech-free. Think of it as hitting the refresh button on your mental health, allowing you to reconnect with yourself and those around you.

Effective screen time management doesn't mean becoming a tech hermit. It's about setting boundaries that allow you to enjoy digital experiences without losing control. Start by *setting screen time limits* on your devices. Most smartphones and tablets come with built-in features that let you track and restrict usage. It's like having a personal trainer for your digital habits, nudging you to put the phone down when you've had enough. Implementing tech-free zones or times at home is another strategy. Whether it's banning screens from the dining table or designating an hour before bed for offline activities, these boundaries create space for genuine connections and relaxation.

Engaging in *offline activities* is not just a suggestion; it's a necessity for a well-rounded life. Hobbies that promote physical and mental well-being offer a break from the digital grind. Whether it's painting, playing an instrument, or taking up gardening, these activities nourish the soul in ways screens cannot. Spending time in nature is especially rejuvenating. The sights, sounds and smells of the great outdoors act as natural stress relievers, boosting your mood and energy levels. It's about creating a tapestry of experiences that enrich your life beyond the confines of a screen.

Parents and guardians play a pivotal role in modeling healthy screen habits. Family dynamics can significantly influence how teens engage with technology. Creating family screen time agreements sets expectations and fosters mutual respect. These agreements might include designated tech-free times or shared activities that don't involve screens. Encouraging open discussions about technology use is equally important. By talking about the benefits and drawbacks of digital media, families can develop a shared understanding and support each other in maintaining balance. It's about leading by example and nurturing a culture where technology enhances rather than dominates life.

Finding balance in a screen-saturated world is not just a personal triumph; it's a family affair. It requires intention, creativity and a bit of humor to keep things light. As you cultivate digital wellness, you're paving the way for a healthier, happier relationship with technology. In the next chapter, we'll explore how these balanced habits can be put into action from a communication and relationship perspective. Ensuring that you develop the skills and confidence to build long-lasting relationships.

MAKE A DIFFERENCE AND GIVE A REVIEW

"The best way to find yourself is to lose yourself in the service of others."

— MAHATMA GANDHI

Your opinion is powerful!

By sharing your thoughts on *'Crucial Life Skills for Teens,'* you're not just reflecting on your own journey; you're giving others the courage and inspiration to begin theirs.

If this book has helped build your self confidence and assisted you in developing skills that will benefit you immediately and for years to come, your story could be the light that someone else needs to make a change. Every review is a ripple that reaches someone who is ready to grow, succeed and thrive.

Why Your Review Matters:

- **Inspire Others:** Your feedback could be the nudge someone needs to invest in themselves and their future.
- **Share Your Wins:** When you highlight what worked for you, you help others see that success is within their reach.
- **Support the Mission:** Your review spreads the messages in Crucial Life Skills For Teens: How To Build Your Self Confidence, Manage Your Money, Live Independently, Overcome Challenges and Achieve Success.

How to Write a Review:

1. **Be Honest:** Share your favorite parts, key takeaways, or how the book made a difference in your life.
2. **Keep It Simple:** A few sentences about what you love is all it takes to make an impact.
3. **Post It Online:** Reviews on Amazon or Goodreads are the best way to help others discover this guide.

We love helping others and hope you will do the same.

Thank you!

   - Freedom Publications: "Your Partner in Personal Growth and Success"

5

COMMUNICATION AND RELATIONSHIP BUILDING

Think of communication as the secret ingredient in the recipe of life. Without it, everything turns bland, like unsalted fries or a joke without a punchline. Communication is the bridge that connects us, allowing us to share ideas, express emotions and build meaningful relationships. It's like a universal translator, capable of turning misunderstandings into connections and tension into trust. Yet, despite its importance, many of us struggle with it, often talking past each other rather than truly engaging.

5.1 COMMUNICATION: AM I COMING IN CLEAR?

One of the most effective ways to enhance communication is through *active listening*. Imagine listening not just with your ears but with your whole being, like a secret agent spy tuning into every whisper and facial twitch, ready to understand and empathize. Active listening is a technique that involves paying full attention to the speaker, interpreting both their words and emotions and responding thoughtfully. According to Carl Rogers, a pioneer of active listening, this approach is essential for effective communication, emphasizing empathy, genuineness and unconditional positive regard. It's like being a communication ninja skilled in the art of understanding and connecting on a deeper level.

Active listening consists of several key elements. First, there's attention, focusing entirely on the speaker without letting your mind wander to what you're having for lunch or whether you left the stove on. Then comes feedback, where you nod or use verbal affirmations like "I see" or "Go on," showing that you're engaged and encouraging the speaker to continue. Summarization is another component where you paraphrase or summarize the speaker's points to ensure understanding. It's like holding up a mirror to reflect what you've heard, confirming that you're on the same page.

Practicing active listening requires some techniques that are as easy as pie once you get the hang of them. Start by paraphrasing and summarizing what the speaker says. If your friend is venting about how their cat knocked over a vase, you might say, "So, you're feeling frustrated because your cat got into some mischief?" This not only shows that you're listening but also helps clarify the speaker's emotions. Maintaining eye contact is crucial, too, as it signals you're present and engaged. Combine this with non-verbal signals like nodding or leaning slightly forward and you're golden.

Of course, barriers to active listening exist, like annoying pop-up ads in the middle of a video. Internal distractions, such as your own thoughts and worries, can pull your focus away from the speaker. Combat this by practicing mindfulness, focusing on the present moment and letting go of distractions. Prejudgments or biases can also get in the way, causing you to filter the speaker's words through your own assumptions. To overcome this, approach each conversation with an open mind, like a blank slate ready to absorb new ideas and perspectives.

The benefits of active listening in relationships are immense, like discovering a hidden treasure chest marked "Trust and Understanding." By truly engaging with others, you build rapport and trust, as the speaker feels heard and valued. This deepens your connection, whether it's with a friend, family member, or colleague. Active listening also enhances conflict resolution abilities, making it easier to navigate disagreements with grace and empathy. When both parties listen actively, they're more likely to find common ground and reach a mutually satisfying resolution.

Interactive Element: Active Listening Exercise

Pair up with a friend or family member and practice active listening. Take turns speaking about a topic of your choice while the other person listens attentively. After a few minutes, the listener should summarize what they heard and reflect any emotions observed. Discuss the experience and how it felt to be truly listened to.

Active listening is a powerful tool that transforms the way we communicate, turning everyday interactions into meaningful exchanges. By honing this skill, you enhance your ability to connect, collaborate and navigate the complexities of human relationships. Whether you're chatting with a friend, resolving a conflict, or simply lending an ear as a sounding board, active listening is your secret weapon for building trust and understanding.

5.2 EXPRESSING YOURSELF: TECHNIQUES FOR EFFECTIVE COMMUNICATION

Clear communication is like a GPS for conversations, guiding you straight to your destination without unnecessary detours. When you express yourself clearly and concisely, you minimize misunderstandings and enhance your interactions. Imagine trying to explain your favorite movie to a friend using only vague gestures and mumbled words; chances are they'd end up more confused than captivated. In contrast, direct communication cuts through the noise like a hot knife through butter, ensuring your message lands precisely as intended. The benefits are plentiful: relationships flourish, conflicts diminish and everyone walks away with a clearer understanding.

Getting your message across effectively requires some structure. Think of your communication as a well-crafted sandwich with a beginning, middle and end. Start by setting the stage and introduce your topic or concern clearly, like the top slice of bread. Next, dive into the heart of your message with the juicy details, like the filling that keeps everything together. Finally, wrap it up with a conclusion or call-to-action, the bottom slice that holds the whole sandwich in place. Using the "I" statement technique is also helpful. Instead of saying, "You never listen," try, "I feel unheard when we talk." This approach reduces defensiveness and makes others more receptive to what you're saying.

But wait, there's more. Tone and body language play pivotal roles in communication. Imagine saying "I'm fine" with a scowl versus a smile, the same words, a totally different vibe. Your tone should match the intent of your message, ensuring your words and emotions align. Meanwhile, body language acts as the exclamation mark that punctuates your sentences. Crossing your arms might suggest defensiveness, while open gestures invite engagement.

Align your body language with your spoken words to reinforce your message and create a more engaging dialogue.

Improving verbal communication skills is akin to tuning an instrument; practice makes perfect and it certainly makes progress. Start by practicing public speaking in small groups. Gather some friends or family, pick a topic and share your thoughts. This exercise helps you refine your articulation and gain confidence. Record and review your speech for self-assessment. Listening to yourself can be cringe-worthy at first, but it's a valuable tool for identifying areas of improvement. You'll notice filler words you might not have realized you used or discover that you tend to rush through certain parts. Use these insights to fine-tune your delivery and become a more effective communicator.

Communication isn't just about what you say; it's about how you say it. The combination of clear content, structured messaging and thoughtful delivery creates a harmonious exchange of ideas. Mastering these techniques can transform your interactions, helping you express yourself with confidence and authenticity. Whether you're presenting in class, chatting with friends, or negotiating curfews with your parents, effective communication is your ticket to success.

5.3 CONFLICT RESOLUTION: TURNING DISAGREEMENTS INTO PRODUCTIVE CONVERSATIONS

Imagine a world where disagreements are solved as easily as a game of rock-paper-scissors. Sadly, life isn't that simple. *Conflict resolution* is crucial for maintaining healthy relationships, whether with family, friends, or coworkers. When handled constructively, conflicts can strengthen bonds rather than weaken them, turning potential disasters into opportunities for growth. Addressing conflicts head-on prevents resentment from simmering beneath the surface, making room for improved understanding and collaboration.

Resolving conflicts isn't rocket science, but it does require a thoughtful approach. Start by identifying the root cause of the disagreement. It's like peeling an onion, sometimes, you have to dig past the surface to find what's truly bothering both parties. Once you pinpoint the issue, seek common ground. Find something you can both agree on, like a shared goal or a mutual interest. It's like finding the common denominator in a math problem; it simplifies the equation. From there, work together to agree on a resolution plan. This step requires collaboration and compromise, ensuring that both parties feel heard and respected.

When tensions rise, it's important to have a toolbox of communication techniques to de-escalate the situation. Active listening is key during disagreements, but let's not dwell on that since we've covered it already. Instead, focus on using "we" statements to foster collaboration. Saying, "We both want to find a solution," is more productive than "You need to change." This subtle shift in language transforms the conversation from a confrontation into a partnership. It's like inviting someone to join you on a team rather than challenging them to a duel.

Empathy is your secret weapon in conflict resolution. By understanding the other person's perspective, you can bridge the gap between disagreement and resolution. This requires stepping into their shoes, seeing the world through their eyes, and recognizing their emotions. Techniques for fostering empathy during disputes include asking open-ended questions and reflecting back on what you've heard. Sharing relatable experiences can also build understanding, as it shows you've faced similar challenges and emotions.

It's like saying, "Hey, I get it. I've been there too," which can make the other person feel less isolated in their frustration.

5.4 BUILDING TRUST: FOUNDATIONS OF STRONG RELATIONSHIPS

Trust is the bedrock of any strong relationship, whether you're talking about friendships, romances, or professional partnerships. It's the invisible glue that holds everything together, allowing people to feel safe and secure in their connections. When trust is present, communication flows more freely and both parties can rely on each other with confidence. Trust isn't built overnight, nor is it a one-time achievement. It requires ongoing effort and nurturing, akin to tending a garden. Elements of trust include reliability, honesty and consistency, like the sturdy three-legged stool that won't wobble under pressure.

Building and maintaining trust involves more than just keeping promises; it's about being transparent and open in communication. Follow through on commitments, and if something goes awry, own up to it. This honesty strengthens trust, showing that you value the relationship enough to be truthful. Being transparent means sharing your thoughts and feelings openly, without hiding behind masks or facades. It's about showing your true self, warts and all, and encouraging others to do the same.

Of course, trust can be shattered, like a fragile vase tumbling off a shelf. When this happens, rebuilding trust involves sincere apologies and demonstrating change through actions. An effective apology acknowledges the impact of your actions, expresses genuine remorse and commits to making amends. Demonstrating change means actively working to prevent similar breaches in the future, like patching up the hole in the metaphorical vase. This process takes time, patience and a willingness to heal and grow together.

In teams and collaborative environments, trust enhances group dynamics, leading to improved cohesion and morale. When team members trust each other, they're more likely to share ideas, support one another and work towards common goals. This trust fuels productivity and innovation, as everyone feels empowered to contribute without fear of judgment or betrayal. It's like having a well-oiled machine, where each part functions smoothly, allowing the whole to perform at its best.

5.5 BUILDING TRUST: FOUNDATIONS OF STRONG RELATIONSHIPS

Trust is the backbone of any relationship, whether it's between friends, family, or colleagues. It's like the Wi-Fi signal that keeps everything connected. When it's strong, you don't even notice it, but when it's weak, everything starts to fall apart. Trust is built on three main pillars: *reliability, honesty, and consistency*. Imagine these as the sturdy legs of a tripod. Without even one, the whole thing topples over. Reliability means showing up when you say you will, like that friend who never bails on movie night. Honesty is about being truthful, even when it's not the easiest route. And consistency? It's doing both of those things regularly enough that people know they can count on you. When these elements come together, they create a solid foundation that supports the weight of the relationship, come rain or shine.

Building and maintaining trust requires intentionality. It's not just about making grand gestures, it's the little things that count. Following through on commitments is crucial. If you promise to help someone with their homework or meet for coffee, do it. Actions speak louder than words and consistently keeping your promises shows you're dependable. Being transparent and open in communication is another vital step. Let's face it: Nobody likes surprises, especially when they pop up as unwanted ads. So, share your thoughts and feelings honestly. If you're struggling with something, say it. If you're excited about something, share it. This openness helps others understand where you're coming from, reducing the chances of misunderstandings.

But what happens when trust is broken? It's like smashing a mirror, rebuilding it takes time and patience. Addressing trust breaches starts with effective and sincere apologies. A *genuine apology* acknowledges the hurt caused, takes responsibility, and expresses remorse. It's not just "I'm sorry you feel that way," but rather, "I'm sorry for what I did." Once you've apologized, it's time to demonstrate change through actions. If you broke trust by being late, start showing up early. If you lied, start being candid, even about small things. These actions rebuild trust over time, like carefully gluing back the pieces of that broken mirror.

Trust doesn't just strengthen personal bonds, it's a game-changer in teamwork and collaboration too. In a group setting, trust boosts cohesion and morale, turning a collection of individuals into a well-oiled machine. When team members trust each other, they feel safe to share ideas, take risks and support one another. This trust fosters an environment where creativity and innovation can flourish. Imagine an orchestra where each musician plays confidently, knowing the others will keep time and hit their notes. Trust is the conductor, guiding everyone toward harmony. Increased productivity naturally follows as team members work together seamlessly, knowing they can count on each other to deliver. It's like adding rocket fuel to a project, propelling it forward with energy and enthusiasm.

5.6 NETWORKING SKILLS: MAKING CONNECTIONS THAT MATTER

Imagine you're at a party where everyone seems to know everyone except you. It's like stepping into a new school and not knowing where to sit at lunch. This is where *networking* comes in. It's the process of building connections that can help you personally and professionally. Whether you're aiming for a summer job, a college recommendation, or just someone to share your love for obscure indie bands, a strong network can open doors you didn't even know existed. Think of your network as a web of relationships, each strand a potential opportunity. The more strands you weave, the more support you build. Networking isn't just for grown-ups in business suits, it's a valuable skill at any age, helping you learn from others, gain insights and maybe even discover your dream path.

So, how do you dive into the world of networking without feeling like you're trying to befriend the entire neighborhood? Start with crafting an *elevator pitch*. This isn't about selling yourself like a used car. It's a brief, engaging summary of who you are, what you're passionate about and what you hope to achieve. Keep it short enough to deliver while riding an elevator, hence the name. Once you've made a connection, following up is key. A quick message or email expressing gratitude for the conversation can work wonders. It not only keeps you fresh in their mind but also shows you're genuinely interested in building a relationship. Networking is like planting seeds with a bit of water (a.k.a. follow-up), they can blossom into fruitful connections.

In today's digital age, *online platforms* are your networking playgrounds. LinkedIn, for example, is like the professional version of social media, where you can showcase your achievements, connect with industry professionals and even discover job opportunities.

Joining *online communities* related to your interests is another great way to expand your network. Whether it's a forum for budding filmmakers or a group for coding enthusiasts, these platforms allow you to connect with like-minded individuals, share knowledge and support each other's growth. Remember, networking isn't just about taking, it's about mutual exchange, where everyone benefits.

But wait, there's an *etiquette* to networking. It's not about shoving business cards into every hand you meet. Maintain *professionalism* in all your interactions, whether online or in person. This means being polite, respectful and attentive. Listen more than you speak and show genuine interest in others' stories and experiences. Expressing gratitude goes a long way, too. Whether someone introduced you to a potential mentor or simply offered valuable advice, a heartfelt thank you can strengthen the bond. Think of networking as a dance; sometimes you lead and sometimes you follow, but it's always about moving together harmoniously.

Networking, therefore, is like building your own support system. It's about connecting with people who can help you grow, learn and succeed.

By honing your networking skills, you're setting yourself up for a future filled with opportunities and collaborations. So, whether you're at a school event, a local meetup, or browsing through LinkedIn, remember that every new connection is a chance to build something meaningful. Embrace the possibilities and you'll find that networking can be as rewarding as it is enjoyable.

5.7 EMPATHY AND COMPASSION: UNDERSTANDING OTHERS' PERSPECTIVES

Imagine walking a mile in someone else's shoes, maybe they're squeaky, or maybe they're too tight. That's *empathy*: the ability to understand and share the feelings of another. It's like a magic mirror reflecting not just your own experiences but also those of others. Empathy allows you to connect on a deeper level, creating bonds that transcend mere words. While empathy involves feeling with someone, *compassion* takes it a step further. It's about recognizing suffering and wanting to alleviate it, like offering a comforting hug or a listening ear. This dynamic duo is crucial in relationships, turning acquaintances into friends and conflicts into collaborations. Unlike sympathy, which might say, "Oh, that's too bad," empathy and compassion sit down beside you and say, "I'm here with you, let's get through this together."

Practicing empathy and compassion might sound like a noble quest, but it's more accessible than you think. Start by truly *listening* to others, not just with your ears but with your heart. When someone shares their struggles, focus on their emotions, understanding what lies beneath their words. Perspective-taking exercises can also enhance your empathetic skills. Imagine how you might feel in a similar situation, and consider the various factors influencing their experience. It's like putting on a pair of glasses that reveal hidden layers of someone's story, offering clarity and understanding. By regularly engaging in these exercises, you build an empathetic mindset that becomes second nature.

Empathy plays a vital role in conflict resolution and collaboration, acting as a bridge over troubled waters. When disputes arise, empathy helps you see beyond your own viewpoint, understanding the concerns and emotions of others. This understanding facilitates better teamwork and problem-solving, as you can work together to find solutions that address everyone's needs. Empathy serves as a tool for mediating disputes, creating an environment where all voices are heard and valued. It fosters collaboration by encouraging open communication and mutual respect. When empathy is present, people are more willing to compromise and support one another, creating a harmonious and productive atmosphere.

Integrating empathy into daily interactions doesn't require grand gestures or heroic feats. It's about small, everyday acts that show you care. Reflect on your own biases and judgments, questioning how they might affect your perception of others. This reflection helps you approach each interaction with an open mind, ready to learn and grow. Celebrate acts of kindness and understanding, both in yourself and in others. Whether it's complimenting a friend, offering help to a stranger, or simply smiling at someone who looks down, these acts ripple through your relationships, spreading warmth and compassion. As empathy becomes a habitual practice, you'll find yourself building stronger connections, fostering a sense of community and belonging.

As we wrap up our exploration of communication and relationship building, remember that *empathy and compassion are the glue that holds everything together.* They transform ordinary interactions into meaningful connections, helping you navigate the complexities of human relationships with grace and understanding. Now, with your newfound skills, you're ready to tackle the challenges of communicating in a digital world, where empathy and compassion are needed more than ever. In the next chapter, we'll explore the importance of effective time management and goal setting, helping you achieve more while feeling less overwhelmed.

6

TIME MANAGEMENT AND GOAL SETTING

Imagine standing in front of a massive buffet table at a party piled high with every dish you could ever dream of. You've got your plate in hand, but there's a catch, your plate is only so big and if you try to pile everything on, you'll end up with a mess on your hands. Time management works a lot like that buffet. There's a whole world of tasks, responsibilities and commitments out there and you have to figure out which ones deserve a spot on your plate. Prioritizing tasks is like deciding which delicious morsels make it to your plate and which ones can wait for second helpings. It's about making sure you focus on what really matters so you don't end up with a pile of soggy, unwanted tasks that leave you overwhelmed.

6.1 HOW TO PRIORITIZE YOUR TIME

Task prioritization is crucial for effective time management and productivity because it allows you to tackle the most important tasks first, ensuring that your limited time and energy are used wisely. Imagine your to-do list as a garden. Without prioritization, it's like planting every seed you have in a tiny plot, hoping for the best. With prioritization, you carefully select which seeds to pant and which plants to nurture, ensuring they get the sunlight and water they need to thrive. By focusing on the essentials, you prevent the overwhelm that comes from trying to do everything at once. Prioritization enhances productivity by directing your attention to high-impact tasks, leaving you with a sense of *accomplishment and clarity.*

There are several techniques to help you identify and focus on these high-impact tasks. One popular method is the *Eisenhower Matrix* (Box/grid), a tool that categorizes tasks based on *urgency and importance*. Picture a simple four-quadrant box. In the top left, you place tasks that are both urgent and important, like finishing a project that's due tomorrow. The top right holds important but not urgent tasks, like planning for a future presentation. The bottom left is for urgent but not important tasks, which you might delegate or handle quickly. The bottom right is for tasks that are neither urgent nor important and these are the ones you can safely ignore or defer. By using this tool, you can visually organize your tasks, making it easier to focus on what truly matters.

Another technique is the *ABCDE prioritization method*. This approach assigns a letter to each task based on its priority level. "A" tasks are top priority and you must complete them today. "B" tasks are important but can wait until "A" tasks are done. "C" tasks are nice to do but not essential. "D" tasks can be delegated, while "E" tasks should be eliminated altogether. This method is like sorting your laundry, "A" tasks are your favorite clothes that need immediate attention, while "E" tasks are the ones you can safely toss or donate. By categorizing tasks this way, you create a clear roadmap for your day, ensuring you tackle the most crucial items first.

Identifying priority tasks involves assessing them based on urgency and importance. Consider *deadlines* and the *consequences* of not completing a task on time. Tasks with looming deadlines or significant repercussions take precedence. But it's not just about urgency, it's also about aligning tasks with your personal and academic goals. Think of your goals as the compass guiding your priorities. If a task aligns with your long-term objectives, it deserves a higher spot on your list.

However, life is unpredictable and *flexibility* is key to prioritization. New tasks may arise, or circumstances may change, requiring you to adapt your priorities. It's like being the captain of a ship, constantly adjusting the sails to navigate the ever-shifting winds. Balancing long-term goals with immediate needs is essential. While it's important to keep your eye on the horizon, don't lose sight of the tasks that require immediate attention. Adjusting priorities as new tasks emerge ensures that you remain agile and responsive, ready to tackle whatever comes your way.

Interactive Element: Prioritization Exercise

Try this: Write down your tasks for the day. Use the Eisenhower Box to categorize them based on urgency and importance. Then, apply the ABCDE method to assign priority levels. Reflect on how these tools help clarify your focus and streamline your day.

By mastering task prioritization, you're not just managing your time, you're taking control of your schedule and setting yourself up for success. Whether you're balancing school assignments, extracurricular activities, or personal projects, prioritizing tasks allows you to focus on what truly matters, leaving you with more time and energy to enjoy the things you love.

6.2 BEATING PROCRASTINATION: STRATEGIES FOR STAYING ON TRACK

Procrastination is the art of convincing yourself that tomorrow is a much better day to start that big project or study for that test. It's like the sneaky villain in your productivity story, whispering sweet nothings about how much more enjoyable scrolling through social media is compared to tackling your to-do list. However, procrastination doesn't just delay tasks; it can wreak havoc on your personal and academic success. When you put off tasks, deadlines sneak up on you, causing *stress, anxiety,* and a mad scramble to complete everything at the last minute. This often results in subpar work and missed opportunities, not to mention the panic-induced caffeine binges.

The causes of procrastination are as varied as the excuses we make for it. Sometimes, it's the fear of failure, where you're so afraid of not getting it right that you don't start at all. Other times, it's the allure of immediate gratification, like watching just one more episode of your favorite show. And let's not forget the overwhelming feeling of not knowing where to begin, which leads to decision paralysis. However, chronic procrastination has consequences. It can damage your reputation, hurt your grades, and lower your self-esteem as tasks pile up and become unmanageable.

To combat procrastination, try the *Pomodoro Technique*, a time management tool that breaks work into 25-minute intervals, known as "pomodoros," with short breaks in between. It's like a game where you race against the clock to get as much done as possible before your time is up. This technique helps maintain focus and turns tasks into manageable chunks, reducing the intimidation factor. Another strategy is breaking tasks into smaller steps. Instead of staring at the monstrous "write essay" task, break it down into "research topic," "outline key points," and "write introduction." Each step becomes a bite-sized task, making it easier to start and complete.

Creating a *productive environment* is crucial. Imagine trying to focus in the middle of a carnival, with chaos, noise and distractions everywhere. Your workspace should be the opposite: a sanctuary of calm. Start by decluttering your workspace. A clear desk equals a clear mind. Implement the "two-minute rule" for quick tasks. If something takes less than two minutes to complete, do it immediately. This rule keeps little tasks from snowballing into bigger ones. A distraction-free zone can significantly enhance your focus, helping you stay on track with your tasks.

Accountability is a powerful motivator in overcoming procrastination. Having someone check in on your progress can push you to stay committed. Consider working with a *study buddy* or an *accountability partner*. It's like having a gym buddy who makes sure you don't skip leg day. Apps that track and reward productivity can also keep you engaged. Some apps 'gamify' your tasks, turning productivity into a competition where you earn points or rewards for completing tasks. These tools make task completion more engaging and enjoyable, providing external motivation to beat procrastination.

Interactive Element: Procrastination Buster Checklist

Create a checklist of small tasks that you've been putting off. Use the "two-minute rule" to tackle each one. Record how many tasks you complete in a day and reflect on how it feels to have them done.

By understanding procrastination and implementing these strategies, you can transform it from a formidable foe into a manageable challenge. You're not just crossing things off a list; you're building skills that will serve you well in school, work, and life.

6.3 CREATING EFFECTIVE SCHEDULES: BALANCING SCHOOL, WORK AND PLAY

Imagine trying to juggle flaming swords while riding a unicycle on a tightrope. That's how life can feel without a well-structured schedule. Balancing school, work and play might seem like an impossible feat, but with the right plan, you can transform chaos into harmony. A balanced schedule is like your personal symphony, where each note hits just right. It's not just about cramming everything in, it's about creating a rhythm that enhances productivity and reduces stress. Having a *routine* helps manage time effectively, allowing you to glide through your day with a sense of purpose. It's like having a reliable GPS that guides you through the twists and turns of daily life, ensuring you don't end up in the dreaded dead-end of stress and missed deadlines.

Designing a *personalized schedule* is your first step toward this harmonious existence. Start by allocating *time blocks* for specific tasks. Think of time blocks as puzzle pieces that fit perfectly into your day, each dedicated to an essential activity, like schoolwork, chores, or even that much-needed Netflix binge. Be sure to incorporate buffer time for unexpected events, because life loves to throw curveballs. It's like leaving room for dessert when you know your grandma's bringing pie, those little buffers save you from the stress of a packed schedule. Remember, your schedule should reflect your unique needs and priorities. Maybe you're a night owl who thrives in the moonlight or an early bird ready to seize the day. Tailor your schedule to fit your natural (Circadian) rhythm so you're not battling against your internal clock.

To keep your schedule on track, enlist the help of digital tools and planners. Apps like *'Google Calendar'* and *'Todoist'* are like your digital sidekicks, helping you manage time with finesse. With Google Calendar, you can set up time blocks and receive reminders, ensuring you never miss a beat. Todoist can organize tasks, providing a satisfying check-off list for those who adore the thrill of ticking boxes. These tools not only keep you organized but also offer a visual representation of your day, which can be as satisfying as a perfectly plated dish. Technology can be a lifesaver, turning your schedule into a well-oiled machine that keeps everything running smoothly.

Flexibility is key to maintaining a schedule without feeling trapped. Life is unpredictable and your schedule should be too. Adjust your plans as priorities shift. Maybe a surprise homework assignment pops up, or your friend's birthday party gets moved to a different day. It's like playing a game of Tetris, where you shift pieces around to keep the lines clear. Implement weekly reviews to reassess your time allocation. Take a moment each week to reflect on what worked and what didn't, making necessary tweaks to stay aligned with your goals. These reviews ensure your schedule remains a living, breathing entity that evolves with you.

Creating a balanced schedule doesn't just help you manage tasks, it enhances your overall well-being. It's like finding that perfect playlist that matches your every mood, making life feel a little more manageable and a lot more enjoyable. With a well-structured schedule, you can navigate your responsibilities with confidence, knowing that you've set yourself up for success. Balancing school, work and play becomes less of a juggling act and more of a graceful dance, allowing you to enjoy every moment without the constant worry of dropping the ball.

6.4 SETTING SMART GOALS: ACHIEVING MORE WITH CLEAR INTENTIONS

Let's think about goals as the GPS coordinates for your life's adventure. Without them, you might end up like a lost tourist, wandering through a world of infinite possibilities without a map to guide you. This is where the concept of *SMART goals* comes in handy, offering a structured framework to set your intentions with precision and purpose. *SMART stands for Specific, Measurable, Achievable, Relevant, and Time-bound.* Each component ensures your goals aren't just dreams floating in the ether but actionable plans grounded in reality. Using this framework enhances goal-setting effectiveness by providing clarity and direction, much like a GPS recalibrating your route to ensure you reach your destination. Imagine setting a goal to "do well in school," a bit vague, right? Now, let's make it SMART: "Increase my math grade from a B to an A by the end of the semester by studying for an hour each day and attending weekly tutoring sessions." It's specific, measurable, achievable, relevant and time-bound, giving you a clear roadmap to follow.

Crafting SMART goals involves a step-by-step process that transforms your aspirations into tangible achievements. Start by defining specific objectives with clarity. Instead of saying, "I want to be healthier," specify, "I will run three miles, three times a week." This precision provides a clear target for which to aim. Next, establish measurable criteria for progress. Without measurement, how will you know if you're on track or need to adjust your approach? If your goal is to save money, set a specific amount, like $500 saved over six months and track your progress. This measurement acts as a thermometer, indicating whether you're heating up or cooling down in your pursuit. Achievability is key, your goals should stretch your capabilities without being impossible. Saving a million dollars by next Tuesday might be a tad ambitious, but setting a realistic savings plan is within reach. Relevance ensures your goals align with your personal values and aspirations. If your goal doesn't resonate with your life's direction, it's like trying to wear shoes two sizes too small, uncomfortable and unsustainable.

However, even the best-laid plans can go awry if you fall into common goal-setting pitfalls. One major mistake is setting unrealistic or overly ambitious goals. While aiming high is admirable, setting unattainable objectives can lead to frustration and burnout. It's like trying to leap over a skyscraper in a single bound, impressive in theory but not achievable in reality. On the flip side, neglecting the relevance of goals to your personal aspirations is another pitfall. Goals should reflect your intrinsic motivations, not external pressures or societal expectations. Otherwise, you risk climbing a ladder only to realize it's leaning against the wrong wall.

Regular *goal reviews* and adjustments are crucial to staying on course. Life is dynamic, and your goals should evolve with changing circumstances. Scheduling regular goal evaluation sessions allows you to assess progress, celebrate successes and make necessary tweaks. It's like adjusting the sails of a ship to catch the wind just right. Did you achieve a milestone sooner than expected? Perhaps it's time to raise the bar and set a new challenge. Conversely, if you're struggling to meet your goals, consider revisiting your strategy and seeking feedback. Progress isn't always linear and setbacks are part of the growth process. Embracing flexibility in your goal-setting journey ensures you remain adaptable and resilient, ready to pivot and recalibrate as needed.

Goal setting isn't just about ticking boxes on a to-do list, it's about crafting a vision for your future and taking intentional steps to make it a reality. Each SMART goal you set is a building block, forming the foundation for your personal and professional growth. With clear intentions and a strategic approach, you'll find yourself achieving more than you ever thought possible. So go ahead, set those SMART goals, and watch as your aspirations transform into accomplishments.

6.5 TRACKING YOUR PROGRESS: TOOLS AND TECHNIQUES FOR SUCCESS

Imagine setting off on a road trip without a map or GPS. You might start out with enthusiasm, but without a way to track your progress, you'll likely end up lost, unsure of how far you've come or how much further you have to go. Tracking your progress toward goals is like having that trusty GPS, providing not only direction but also motivation and insights for improvement. When you *visualize your progress*, it's like watching an empty gas tank slowly fill up, showing you that the finish line is closer than you think. This visualization keeps your spirits high and your motivation fueled, especially on those days when your goals feel like they're miles away.

One effective way to track your goals and tasks is through *bullet journaling*. This creative yet structured method allows you to organize your thoughts, tasks and progress in one place. Imagine a journal that's as colorful and personal as a scrapbook but as organized as a spreadsheet. You get to design each page, tracking daily tasks, weekly goals, or even mood and habit trackers. This method not only provides a comprehensive overview of your progress but also offers a therapeutic outlet for creativity. For those more digitally inclined, apps like 'Habitica' take tracking to another level by gamifying the process. Again, it's like turning your life into a video game, where completing tasks earns you points and rewards, adding a fun twist to productivity. These tools help you stay on track, making progress visible and tangible.

Feedback plays a crucial role in refining strategies and enhancing performance. Think of it like a friendly nudge from a coach on the sidelines, helping you adjust your approach and improve your game. *Constructive feedback* from peers, mentors, or teachers provides valuable insights into what's working and what needs tweaking. It's like having a second pair of eyes that might see opportunities for improvement you hadn't noticed. Self-reflection is another powerful tool for personal growth. Taking time to reflect on your actions, successes and setbacks allows you to learn from your experiences, helping you grow and adapt. It's like pausing to read the manual before assembling furniture, you gain clarity and direction, reducing the risk of mistakes.

Accountability is the glue that holds your progress-tracking efforts together. Sharing your goals and progress with others reinforces commitment and keeps you motivated. Whether it's joining an accountability group or sharing updates with a mentor, having someone to check in with can boost your determination. Imagine you're climbing a mountain, having a buddy along makes the climb not only more manageable but also more enjoyable. Participating in forums or groups dedicated to shared goals can provide a sense of community and support, turning what might feel like a solitary endeavor into a collective journey. This shared accountability acts as a safety net, catching you when you stumble and cheering you on as you reach new heights.

Visual Element: Progress Tracking Chart

Create a chart that maps out your progress toward a specific goal. Use colors to represent different stages or *milestones*. Display it somewhere visible to serve as a constant reminder of how far you've come.

Tracking progress is more than just a method for measuring success. It's an invaluable tool that keeps you *focused, motivated* and *adaptable* as you work toward your goals. With the right techniques and tools, you can ensure that each step you take is a step in the right direction, leading you closer to your ultimate destination.

6.6 CELEBRATING MILESTONES: MOTIVATING YOURSELF TO KEEP GOING

Imagine climbing a mountain. Each step is an effort, every muscle strains, but reaching the summit rewards you with a breathtaking view. *Celebrating* achievements is like that moment when you reach the top and shout, "I did it!" *Recognizing accomplishments* isn't just about the joy of reaching a goal, it's a powerful motivator that fuels your next climb. It boosts morale, reinforces positive behaviors and provides a psychological boost that makes the journey ahead feel less daunting. When you celebrate success, you're telling yourself, "Hey, you're pretty amazing!" This acknowledgment not only uplifts your spirits but also strengthens your resolve to keep pushing forward.

Determining which milestones are worth celebrating is crucial. Not every step needs a parade, but significant goal markers and overcoming major obstacles certainly deserve recognition. Think of it as throwing a mini-party for your progress. Did you finally finish that research paper you've been chipping away at for weeks? Or maybe you tackled a fear that's been holding you back, like speaking in front of a group. These are the moments to pause and give yourself a high-five. Celebrating doesn't have to be grandiose, it's about acknowledging the effort and growth that brought you there. This practice reinforces the behaviors and habits that lead to success, creating a *positive feedback loop* that encourages further achievement.

Now, let's get creative with celebrations. Forget the usual cake and balloons, think outside the box. Establish a personal reward system where each milestone earns you a treat, perhaps a new book, a day trip, or even a guilt-free lazy day. Organize *milestone celebrations* with friends or family. Share your victories, big or small, with those who cheer you on. It's like throwing confetti on your journey, adding bursts of joy that make the process more enjoyable. Celebrations create memories that anchor your achievements, giving you something to look back on with pride.

Reflection is another key aspect of celebrating success. Maintaining a success journal helps you track achievements and reflect on the journey. It's like a scrapbook of your progress, filled with lessons learned, obstacles overcome and goals achieved. Writing about your successes allows you to internalize them, turning fleeting moments into lasting insights. Sharing your learnings and experiences with peers can also be enlightening. It's like swapping stories around a campfire, where everyone gains from each other's adventures. These reflections inspire future efforts by highlighting what works and what doesn't, providing a roadmap for your next endeavor.

As we wrap up this chapter, remember that celebrating milestones isn't just about the destination, it's about appreciating the journey. Each victory, no matter how small, is a stepping stone that propels you forward. Recognizing these moments encourages continued growth and perseverance. Next, we'll explore self-discovery and personal growth, diving into the fascinating realm of understanding yourself and your unique potential.

7

SELF-DISCOVERY AND PERSONAL GROWTH

7.1 WHO DO YOU WANT TO BE ?

Imagine walking into a library where each book represents a unique talent waiting to be discovered and read. Some books are in plain sight, ready to be picked up, while others are hidden on dusty top shelves, needing a little more effort to reach. Just like that library, each of us is filled with hidden *talents and abilities* that are waiting to be unearthed. Recognizing your talents isn't just about finding a hidden gem, it's about understanding and embracing what makes you, well, you. These talents propel you toward personal fulfillment and success, much like finding a book that speaks to your soul. They can boost your self-esteem, improve your sense of purpose and guide you toward future career paths that resonate with your true self.

Realizing what you're good at can be a game-changer. It's like finding that perfect pair of jeans that make you feel amazing every time you wear them. Discovering and honing your talents can significantly enhance *self-esteem,* providing a solid foundation to build *confidence* and *resilience*. When you know your strengths, you're more likely to pursue opportunities that align with them, leading to greater satisfaction and success. Just think about it, if you're naturally gifted at playing the guitar, wouldn't you feel more fulfilled strumming your way through life rather than trying to master something that doesn't spark the same joy? Aligning your talents with your *career choices* is like setting your antenna to happiness, you're bound to end up in a place that feels right for you.

So, how do you dig up these hidden talents? Start by taking *personality and aptitude tests*, which are like treasure maps pointing you toward potential strengths. These tests can reveal insights into your personality traits, interests and skills you might not even realize you possess. Reflecting on past accomplishments and *feedback* from others can also provide valuable clues. What activities do you lose track of time doing? What skills have you been praised for at school or at work? Your talents often reside in the things you love to do and excel at without even trying. Think of these reflections as piecing together a puzzle, with each piece revealing a bit more about what makes you unique.

Once you've unearthed your talents, it's time to polish and refine them. Enrolling in *workshops* or classes can provide the structured learning environment needed to develop your skills further. Whether it's improving your painting technique or learning advanced coding, these opportunities allow you to dive deeper into your interests. Seeking mentorship from skilled professionals can also be invaluable. A *mentor* can offer guidance, share their experiences and help you navigate challenges along the way. Imagine having a wise owl by your side, pointing you in the right direction and cheering you on as you soar to new heights.

Experimentation is key to talent discovery. Just like trying out different flavors of ice cream, you never know what you might love until you give it a go. Participating in *clubs or extracurricular activities* exposes you to new experiences and helps you uncover hidden talents. Whether it's joining the drama club and discovering a knack for acting or signing up for a coding class and finding out you're a whiz with computers, these activities provide a safe space to explore and grow. Volunteering for diverse experiences can also broaden your horizons, offering the chance to apply your skills in real-world situations. Plus, it feels great to give back to the community while learning more about yourself.

Interactive Element: Talent Reflection Exercise

Grab a notebook and jot down three activities that make you lose track of time. Next, think of a recent compliment or positive feedback you've received and write that down, too. Reflect on how these might point to your talents. Consider how you might explore and nurture these further.

By delving into your talents and embracing what you discover, you're taking a significant step toward personal growth and self-discovery. You'll find that understanding your unique abilities not only enriches your own life but also allows you to contribute positively to the lives of others.

7.2 IDENTIFYING YOUR VALUES: WHAT TRULY MATTERS TO YOU

Imagine you're building a house. The foundation you choose determines its strength and stability. *Personal values* are like that foundation, guiding principles that shape your decisions and behaviors, much like a compass pointing you in the right direction.

They influence how you navigate challenges, interact with others, and pursue your goals. Values are those invisible forces that steer your life, ensuring you remain true to yourself amidst the noise of the world. When your values align with your actions, you experience a sense of life satisfaction and fulfillment, like slipping into a pair of shoes that fit just right. Without them, you might find yourself wandering aimlessly, questioning every decision like a contestant on a game show with no lifelines.

Values also play a crucial role in guiding ethical decisions, helping you distinguish right from wrong. Think of them as your personal moral conscience, prompting you to recalculate your route when you stray off course. They provide a framework for evaluating choices, ensuring they align with your core beliefs. This alignment helps you make decisions with confidence, knowing they reflect who you are and what you stand for. When faced with dilemmas, your values act as a steadfast anchor, preventing you from drifting into murky waters. Imagine, for instance, being offered a job that pays well but conflicts with your environmental values. Understanding what's truly important to you helps you quickly assess such tricky situations, keeping you steady on your chosen path.

Uncovering your core values is like embarking on a treasure hunt, with the prize being a deeper understanding of yourself. *Reflective journaling* prompts can help you dig beneath the surface, uncovering what truly matters to you. Ask yourself questions like, "What brings me joy?" or "What principles do I hold dear, even when no one is watching?" By exploring these questions, you begin to paint a picture of your values, much like an artist bringing a blank canvas to life. Values clarification exercises are another tool in this quest, offering a structured approach to identifying your priorities. They involve selecting words from a list that resonate with you and then reflecting on why these values are significant. This process can feel like a revelation, shedding light on the intricate web of beliefs that make you uniquely you.

Your values profoundly impact your relationships and goals. They shape the interactions you have with others, influencing the friendships you form and the boundaries you set. Aligning friendships with shared values creates a strong foundation for meaningful connections, like building a house on solid ground. When you share similar values with friends, you create an environment of mutual understanding and respect where you can grow and thrive together. Values also guide you in setting goals that reflect your true desires and aspirations. They help you prioritize what's important, ensuring your goals are aligned with your vision for life. This alignment brings a sense of purpose and direction, making the pursuit of your goals feel like a natural extension of who you are.

Living authentically according to your values involves integrating them into your daily life. It's about making decisions that align with your beliefs, much like choosing clothes that fit your style. Creating a *personal values statement* can serve as a guiding star, reminding you of what matters most. This statement acts as a touchstone, helping you stay true to your values when faced with life's challenges. By consistently reflecting on your values and allowing them to guide your actions, you cultivate a life of authenticity and integrity. You become like a skilled sailor, navigating the seas with confidence, knowing your compass is set to true north.

Textual Element: Values Reflection Section

Take a moment to write down three core values that resonate with you. Reflect on how these values influence your decisions, relationships and goals. Consider moments when you've acted in alignment with these values and times when you've strayed. How did each situation make you feel? Use these reflections to craft a personal values statement, a succinct expression of what truly matters to you. Keep this statement visible as a reminder to guide your choices and actions.

By embracing your values and letting them shape your life, you create a tapestry of experiences that reflects your true self. In a world that often demands conformity, staying true to your values is a courageous act, a declaration of your identity and purpose. It's like dancing to your own rhythm, creating a symphony of authenticity that resonates with every step you take.

7.3 BUILDING CONFIDENCE: OVERCOMING SELF-DOUBT AND FEAR

Imagine standing on a stage, spotlight shining and instead of feeling like a rabbit caught in headlights, you're owning that moment with unwavering confidence. *Building self-confidence* is like constructing a sturdy bridge that carries you over the turbulent waters of self-doubt and fear. It's the secret sauce that not only propels you in social settings but also bolsters your academic achievements. Confidence allows you to approach situations with a mindset of "I can" rather than "Can I?" Whether it's giving a presentation or simply speaking up in class, confidence acts as your backstage pass to opportunities you might otherwise shy away from. As you cultivate this inner strength, you find yourself bouncing back from setbacks more easily, like a spring-loaded action figure ready to tackle life's challenges head-on.

To kick self-doubt to the curb, start by challenging those pesky negative self-perceptions. *Positive self-affirmations* are your superhero cape. Instead of telling yourself, "I'm not good enough," try, "I am capable and ready to learn." These affirmations reinforce positive beliefs about yourself and gradually shift your mindset. Pair this with visualizing successful outcomes. Picture yourself acing that exam or nailing that interview. Visualization is like rehearsing for the big performance, helping you feel more prepared and less anxious. And remember, practicing self-compassion is crucial. Treat yourself like you would a friend in need, with kindness and understanding, especially when things don't go as planned.

Confidence isn't built overnight; it's a series of small, attainable victories that stack up over time. Set goals that are just a notch above your comfort zone. Maybe it's speaking up once in every class or trying out for a school play. Celebrate these triumphs, no matter how small. Did you finally ask that question in class? High-five yourself! Each step you take is a building block in your confidence castle. Stepping out of your comfort zone is like dipping your toes into a cold pool. At first, it's uncomfortable; you have to adjust, but soon, you'll be swimming with ease. The more you challenge yourself, the more you realize how capable you truly are.

Now, let's talk about the power of *body language*. Your physical presence can influence not only how others perceive you but also how you perceive yourself. Ever heard of power posing? It's the idea that standing in a confident posture, like a superhero with hands on hips, can actually boost your confidence. Studies suggest that holding such poses for just a couple of minutes can increase feelings of power and reduce stress. And don't underestimate the impact of eye contact. Maintaining eye contact during conversations shows you're engaged and confident, making others more likely to listen and respond positively. Plus, it helps you connect on a deeper level, like a Wi-Fi signal that's finally strong enough for uninterrupted streaming.

Confidence is your ticket to exploring new opportunities, making meaningful connections and achieving your goals. It's not about being fearless, it's about acknowledging your fears and choosing to act anyway. So, next time you find yourself doubting your abilities, remember to stand tall, speak kindly to yourself, and take that leap. With each step, you'll find your confidence growing, ready to take on the world.

7.4 FINDING YOUR PASSION: PURSUING WHAT YOU LOVE

Imagine waking up every day with that electric feeling of excitement buzzing in your chest, ready to tackle whatever comes your way. That's the magic of pursuing your passions. *Passion* isn't just a hobby you enjoy on weekends, it's the driving force that fuels your motivation and engagement in everything you do. When you're passionate about something, whether it's baking, coding, or playing the ukulele, you dive deep, lose track of time and emerge feeling energized and fulfilled. Passion acts like a magnetic compass, guiding your career choices and steering you towards paths that align with what you love. We all know life's too short to spend it on things that make you groan every Monday morning. Instead, let passion be your guide, leading you to a life filled with purpose and joy.

Finding what sets your soul on fire often requires a bit of exploration. Start by dipping your toes into diverse activities and hobbies. Think of it as sampling every dish at a buffet. How else would you know which ones you crave more? Try your hand at painting, take a dance class, or learn to speak Klingon (hey, you never know!). Reflect on moments when you felt the most alive, when time seemed to fly by, and everything just clicked. These are your moments of flow, where passion thrives. They serve as clues, pointing you toward interests that resonate with your core.

Following your passion isn't just about personal satisfaction, it opens doors to growth and opportunities. When you're passionate, you naturally invest time and effort into building expertise. You become the go-to person on that subject, like the friend everyone calls when they need a recipe for the best brownies ever. This expertise not only boosts your confidence but also creates avenues for meaningful work. Whether it's turning your passion for photography into a career or using your love for animals to volunteer at a shelter, pursuing your interests can lead to a fulfilling professional life.

Integrating your passions into daily life doesn't have to be daunting. It can be as simple as starting a blog or a YouTube channel that focuses on something you're passionate about. Share your knowledge, experiences and the occasional blooper reel, connecting with others who share your enthusiasm. Joining interest-based communities or clubs also offers a sense of belonging and inspiration. Whether it's a local gardening group or an online forum for aspiring writers, these communities provide support and encouragement, making the journey more enjoyable. Passion projects, big or small, breathe life into your routine, filling your days with creativity and purpose.

Interactive Element: Passion Exploration Exercise

Grab a notebook or open a notes app. Spend a few minutes writing down activities that excite you or topics you love to discuss. Reflect on your "flow moments," times when you felt completely absorbed in what you were doing. Highlight any recurring themes or interests. Consider how you might explore these further or incorporate them into your life. Whether it's joining a club, taking a class, or starting a project, let your passions guide you toward new adventures.

7.5 CREATING A VISION BOARD: VISUALIZING YOUR FUTURE

Picture a corkboard filled with vibrant images, inspiring quotes and tokens that represent your dreams. That's a vision board, a literal collage of your aspirations. It's like having a personal billboard of your goals right there in your room. Vision boards are more than just arts and crafts, they're powerful tools that help you focus and motivate yourself through visualization. By seeing your ambitions displayed daily, you reinforce your commitment to them, much like a coach rallying their team with a pep talk. They serve as a visual reminder of what you're striving for, making it easier to keep your goals top of mind and stay motivated even on those days when your bed feels like a magnet.

Creating an effective vision board is a fun and creative process. Start by gathering images and quotes that ignite a spark in you. These could be cutouts from magazines, printouts from the internet, or even your own drawings. The key is to choose visuals that resonate deeply with your dreams and ambitions. Once you have your materials, organize them by themes or goals. Maybe you want to travel, excel in school, or become a maestro on the piano. Grouping your aspirations makes them feel more tangible and less like a scattered wishlist. Arrange them in a way that's pleasing to your eye, after all, you'll be seeing this board every day!

Visualization plays a crucial role in achieving your goals. When you consistently see what you're aiming for, it becomes easier to visualize the steps needed to get there. This mental rehearsal can enhance motivation and focus, acting as a dress rehearsal for success. By picturing yourself reaching your goals, you're more likely to spot opportunities and take actions that align with your dreams. Daily visualization practices, even if just for a few minutes, can be incredibly powerful. Try incorporating visualization into your routine by taking a moment each morning to imagine what achieving your goals feels like. It's like giving your brain a morning coffee boost but without the caffeine jitters.

Of course, a vision board isn't a static piece of art. It's a living document that evolves as you grow and change. Regularly reviewing and updating your board keeps it relevant and inspiring. As you achieve goals, celebrate by adding new ones. This dynamic process helps maintain your enthusiasm and commitment. Think of it like updating your playlist with new tracks that keep you pumped and ready to face the day. Periodically, take time to assess your progress and reflect on what's working and what's not. This reflection can offer valuable insights, ensuring your board remains a true reflection of where you want to go.

Creating a vision board is a personal and empowering experience. It's a way to take charge of your future, turning your dreams into actionable goals. Plus, it's a chance to let your creativity shine as you design something uniquely yours. So grab some magazines, scissors and a glue stick and get started on crafting your vision. It's not just about dreaming, it's about daring to make those dreams a reality.

7.6 JOURNALING FOR PERSONAL GROWTH: REFLECTING ON YOUR JOURNEY

Imagine cracking open a blank notebook and letting your thoughts spill out like a river breaking free from a dam. That's journaling, a simple yet powerful practice that enhances self-awareness and reflection. It's like having a conversation with yourself, minus the awkward silence. The benefits of journaling are vast, offering psychological perks like reduced stress and improved problem-solving. When you put pen to paper, you're creating a safe space to process emotions, much like a personal therapist available 24/7. Regular journaling can lead to greater insights, helping you understand the 'whys' behind your thoughts and actions, ultimately guiding you toward personal growth.

Now, you might wonder how to start journaling effectively. One approach is gratitude journaling, where you jot down things that make you thankful each day. This practice shifts your focus from what's lacking to what's abundant, making gratitude your new best friend. Reflecting on daily experiences and learnings is another technique. Consider what went well, what didn't, and what you learned. It's like a mental debrief, helping you make sense of your day and uncovering patterns over time. Whether it's a lesson learned from a mistake or a moment of joy, writing it down reinforces your growth and development.

Journaling isn't one-size-fits-all, so explore various methods until you find your groove. *Bullet journaling* is perfect for those who crave organization. It combines to-do lists, calendars and reflections in a streamlined format, making it easy to keep track of your life. It's like having a personal assistant in notebook form. On the flip side, *freewriting* is for the free spirits. It involves writing continuously without worrying about grammar or structure, letting your thoughts flow like an unfiltered stream. This method encourages creativity and spontaneity, allowing you to explore ideas without self-censorship. Both approaches offer unique ways to engage with your thoughts and emotions, catering to different preferences.

To make journaling a consistent habit, integrate it into your daily routine. Set aside a dedicated time, perhaps in the morning with your coffee or before bed, as a wind-down ritual. This regularity turns journaling into a rewarding habit, like brushing your teeth, but way more insightful. Whether you choose a physical notebook or a journaling app, find a medium that resonates with you. Some people love the tactile experience of pen on paper, while others prefer the convenience and portability of digital tools. Whatever you choose, let it be a space where you can freely express yourself without fear or judgment.

Interactive Element: Gratitude Journaling Prompt

Grab your journal and write down three things you're grateful for today. They can be as simple as a sunny day or as profound as a supportive friend. Reflect on why these things matter to you and how they positively impact your life. Notice how this exercise shifts your perspective and enhances your well-being.

As we wrap up this chapter, consider how journaling can be your personal roadmap, guiding you through life's twists and turns. It's a tool for self-discovery, helping you reflect on where you've been and where you want to go. With each entry, you cultivate a deeper understanding of yourself, paving the way for growth and transformation. Now, let's turn the page and explore how these insights can empower you to navigate future challenges.

8

PREPARING FOR THE FUTURE: CAREER PLANNING AND BEYOND

Imagine wandering through a bustling bazaar, each stall offering a glimpse into a different life path, some familiar, others as exotic as a camel in a top hat. This bazaar is your career landscape and exploring it early can set the stage for a future as bright as a neon sign at midnight. Career exploration isn't just about picking a job, it's about discovering who you are, what you love, and how you can contribute to the world. Understanding potential career paths early on helps you make informed educational and professional decisions, leading to a life filled with purpose and satisfaction. Aligning your career with personal interests means waking up excited for the day, not just for the weekend. It's about finding a role that feels less like work and more like a calling.

8.1 WHICH WAY SHOULD YOU GO?

To begin this adventure, you might want to start by identifying your personal interests and strengths. It's like being a detective in your own life, piecing together clues from the hobbies and activities that bring you joy. Interest inventories and career quizzes can be your magnifying glass, revealing patterns and preferences you might not have noticed before. Ever felt a spark while tinkering with gadgets or peace while helping others? These moments are hints pointing toward potential career paths. Reflecting on what you do in your free time, whether it's coding, crafting, or analyzing the lyrics of your favorite song, can offer insights into your natural inclinations.

Once you have a better grasp of your interests, it's time to explore the vast resources available for *career exploration*. Informational interviews with professionals in fields that intrigue you can be eye-opening. It's like getting the inside scoop on a movie before it hits the theaters. Asking questions about their daily tasks, challenges and rewards can help you envision yourself in their role. Additionally, platforms like 'O*NET' and 'My Next Move' offer detailed information about various careers, from job descriptions to salary expectations. They're like virtual libraries, packed with the knowledge you need to make informed choices.

Real-world experiences such as *internships and job shadowing* are invaluable for gaining insights into potential careers. Think of them as test drives for your future, low-commitment opportunities to experience the reality of a profession. Finding local internship opportunities can be as simple as reaching out to companies you're interested in or utilizing school resources. Job shadowing, where you observe professionals at work, provides a behind-the-scenes look at the industry. It's like peeking backstage at a concert, seeing the magic behind the performance. These experiences can confirm your interests or steer you in a new direction, ensuring you're on the path that truly resonates with you.

Interactive Element: Career Exploration Checklist

Create a checklist to guide your career exploration journey. Include tasks like taking interest inventories, scheduling informational interviews, researching on O*NET, and identifying potential internships or job shadowing opportunities. Use this checklist to track your progress and reflect on what you discover along the way.

By starting this exploration early, you equip yourself with the tools and insights needed to navigate the career bazaar confidently. It's a journey of self-discovery, where each step brings you closer to a future full of possibilities.

8.2 RESUME BUILDING: CRAFTING A STANDOUT CV

Picture this, you're about to audition for the role of a lifetime, but instead of a stage, you're facing a desk. Your *resume* is your script, your chance to shine. It's more than just a piece of paper, it's your personal billboard, highlighting your skills, achievements and potential. In the world of job applications, a well-crafted resume is your golden ticket, opening doors to interviews and opportunities that can shape your future. It's your first impression on potential employers, who often make snap judgments based on the polish and professionalism of your resume. This makes crafting an effective resume not just important but crucial in distinguishing yourself from a sea of applicants.

The anatomy of a standout resume isn't as complex as dissecting a frog in biology class, but it does require some precision. Start with your contact information at the top and make sure your email address is professional (save the quirky ones for personal use). Follow with a professional summary, a brief paragraph that sums up your experience and goals, whetting the employer's appetite for more. When detailing your education, include relevant coursework that shows off your brainpower and dedication. For work experience, highlight not just what you did but what you achieved. If you've held part-time jobs, volunteered, or led any projects, this is your chance to brag a little. Remember, each bullet point should tell a story of responsibility and initiative. Volunteer activities count too, employers love seeing community involvement.

Just like you wouldn't wear flip-flops to a black-tie event, you shouldn't send a one-size-fits-all resume. *Tailoring your resume* to match the job description is key. This means using *keywords* from the job posting, think of them as the secret code that gets your resume noticed by applicant tracking systems. Highlight relevant skills and experiences that align with the role. If you're applying for a graphic design position, emphasize your creativity and design software skills. For a customer service role, showcase your communication and problem-solving abilities. Customizing your resume shows employers you're genuinely interested in the role, not just blasting out applications like confetti.

Of course, even the most dazzling resume can be dimmed by common mistakes. Avoid cluttering your resume with irrelevant information; every word should serve a purpose. Keep it concise and focused. Watch out for typos and grammatical errors, the unwelcome party crashers of any resume. Proofread meticulously, or better yet, have a friend review it. An extra pair of eyes can catch mistakes you might overlook. Presentation matters, too, use a clean, easy-to-read format and stick to one page. Remember, your resume is a reflection of you, so make sure it's neat and professional. It's even worth considering using a professional resume writer or a resume writing service. You could start by searching a site such as Fiverr to find one.

These tips are your toolkit for building a resume that stands out like a beacon in a foggy sea of applications. With a polished resume in hand, you're ready to step into the world of job hunting with confidence, knowing that your skills and experiences are showcased in the best possible light.

8.3 THE JOB INTERVIEW: PRESENTING YOURSELF WITH CONFIDENCE

Imagine the job interview as the grand stage where you get to be the star of your own show. It's your chance to let your personality and skills shine brighter than a disco ball at a school dance. Interviews are pivotal in the hiring process because they allow employers to see beyond the resume and evaluate how well you fit within their team. It's not just about listing your accomplishments; it's about building a connection with the interviewer and showing them you're more than just a list of bullet points. Preparation is your best friend here, helping you feel as calm and collected as a yogi meditating on a mountaintop.

Preparing for interviews can feel like a daunting task, but breaking it down by format can help. Traditional in-person interviews are like a face-to-face conversation where your handshake and smile matter just as much as your answers. Dress appropriately, exude confidence and remember to breathe. Telephone and video interviews, on the other hand, might seem less intimidating since you can wear pajama pants off-screen, but they require clear communication. Practice speaking clearly and find a quiet space with a reliable internet connection. Group or panel interviews can feel like facing a firing squad, but they're really just an opportunity to demonstrate your ability to engage multiple personalities at once. Maintain eye contact with all panel members and address their questions with equal poise.

To turn the interview into a smashing success, practice your interview skills. Go over common interview questions and rehearse your responses until they roll off your tongue like your favorite song lyrics. Think about questions like "Tell me about yourself," "What are your strengths and weaknesses?" and "Why do you want this job?" Use the *STAR method* (Situation, Task, Action, Result) for behavioral questions, which helps you structure your answers into compelling narratives. For example, if asked about teamwork, describe a time when you faced a group project, the role you played, the actions you took to ensure success and the positive outcome. This method paints a vivid picture of your capabilities, making it easier for interviewers to visualize your potential contributions.

Once the interview is over, don't just drop the mic and walk away. Post-interview etiquette is crucial for leaving a lasting impression. Sending a thank-you email within 24 hours is a small gesture with a big impact. Express gratitude for the opportunity and briefly reiterate your enthusiasm for the position. This simple act can reinforce your interest and professionalism, setting you apart from other candidates who may skip this step altogether. Reflecting on your interview performance is another useful exercise. Think about what went well and areas where you could improve. Did you stumble on a particular question? Were you as concise as you intended to be? Use these reflections to enhance your skills for future interviews.

Remember, interviews are not just about finding the right job; they're about finding the right fit for you. Be authentic, showcase your true self and view each interview as a learning experience. Whether you land the job or not, each interview brings you closer to the right opportunity.

8.4 NETWORKING FOR TEENS: BUILDING PROFESSIONAL RELATIONSHIPS EARLY

Networking might sound like a buzzword your parents throw around at dinner parties, but it's actually a powerful tool that can open doors to a world of opportunities. Think of networking as building bridges between you and the people who can help you along your career path. It's not just about collecting business cards or adding connections on LinkedIn. It's about forming genuine relationships that can provide advice, support and possibly even job leads. Networking allows you to tap into a pool of knowledge and experience that can guide your decisions, helping you navigate your career with the wisdom of those who've walked the path before you.

Getting started with networking as a teen might feel a bit like trying to join a game mid-play, but it's not as daunting as it seems. One of the easiest ways to kick off your networking journey is by joining school clubs and organizations. These groups are excellent platforms to meet like-minded peers who share your interests. Whether it's the robotics club, debate team, or art society, being active in these environments not only hones your skills but also connects you with people who might share valuable insights or opportunities. Attending career fairs and workshops is another fantastic way to meet professionals and learn about various industries. These events often feature guest speakers and panels, offering a chance to hear firsthand about different career paths.

In today's digital age, online networking plays a crucial role in expanding your professional circle. Creating a *LinkedIn profile* is a great starting point for establishing your professional presence online. It's like a digital resume that allows you to showcase your skills, accomplishments and interests to potential employers and mentors. Engaging with industry-specific online groups can also be beneficial. Platforms like *LinkedIn, Reddit, or even Facebook* host groups where professionals discuss trends, share advice, and post job openings. Participating in these communities can provide you with valuable insights and opportunities to connect with individuals in your field of interest.

Maintaining professional relationships requires a bit of effort, but the rewards are well worth it. Regularly reaching out to your contacts helps keep the connection alive. This doesn't mean you have to bombard them with messages, but a simple check-in or sharing an article you think they'd find interesting can go a long way. It shows that you value the relationship and are thinking of them, even if it's just to say, "Hey, I found this and thought of you!" Building a strong network is about creating lasting, meaningful relationships that can support you throughout your career, not just transactional exchanges.

Visual Element: Networking Map

Create a *visual map* of your current network, including school contacts, family friends and online connections. Identify potential gaps and think about how you might expand your network in those areas. Use this map to set *networking goals*, like reaching out to someone new each month or attending a specific event.

Networking isn't just about getting your foot in the door, it's about building a foundation for your future. As you meet new people and learn from their experiences, you'll find yourself better prepared to tackle the challenges and opportunities that come your way.

8.5 CONTINUOUS LEARNING: STAYING CURIOUS AND OPEN TO NEW EXPERIENCES

Imagine your brain as a sponge. It soaks up knowledge and the more you feed it, the more it grows. Lifelong learning is the key to keeping that sponge nice and plump, ready to tackle whatever challenges life throws your way. In today's rapidly shifting job market, skills can become outdated faster than you can say "vintage." Continuous education and skill development are crucial for staying relevant and competitive. As industries evolve, so must you. Adapting to these changes means you're not just surviving, you're thriving, turning every hurdle into a stepping stone toward career success.

Now, where do you find these learning opportunities? The world is your classroom, and the *internet* is the ultimate library card. Online courses and certifications are a fantastic way to dive into new subjects without leaving your couch. Platforms like 'Coursera,' 'Udemy' and 'Khan Academy' offer courses ranging from coding to culinary arts. If you're more of a hands-on learner, attending workshops and seminars can be enlightening. These gatherings provide a chance to engage with experts, ask questions and meet others who share your passion for growth. Whether online or in person, these resources are invaluable for expanding your knowledge and sharpening your skills.

But don't stop there. Why not explore diverse fields and subjects? A multidisciplinary approach to learning is like having a Swiss Army knife in your brain. Taking elective courses outside your major or dabbling in hobbies that develop new skills can open doors you never knew existed. Maybe you're a budding engineer with a secret love for painting or a future doctor who enjoys writing poetry. These seemingly unrelated interests can enrich your primary focus, offering fresh perspectives and innovative ideas. Who knows? That art class might just inspire the next big engineering breakthrough or medical discovery.

Curiosity is the rocket fuel for both personal and professional growth. It's the little voice that asks, "What if?" and "Why not?" Cultivating a curious mindset means constantly asking questions and seeking knowledge. It's about embracing challenges as learning opportunities rather than obstacles to avoid. This mindset fuels innovation and creativity, allowing you to see problems as puzzles waiting to be solved. By staying curious, you keep your mind agile, ready to adapt and innovate in any situation. Whether you're figuring out how to fix a leaky faucet or brainstorming the next big startup idea, curiosity is your best ally.

Textual Element: Curiosity Challenge

Take on a curiosity challenge: commit to learning about one new topic each week, whether it's a scientific concept, a historical event, or a different culture. Document your findings in a journal, reflecting on how each new piece of knowledge broadens your perspective.

Continuous learning isn't just a duty, it's an adventure. Each new skill is a tool, each new idea a stepping stone. Embrace the ever-changing landscape of knowledge with open arms and watch as it transforms your life in ways you never imagined.

8.6 GIVING BACK: VOLUNTEERING AND CONTRIBUTING TO YOUR COMMUNITY

Picture this: you're part of a community that hums with the collective energy of people coming together like a well-rehearsed orchestra. Volunteering is your ticket to this symphony, where each note represents acts of kindness and service that enhance personal growth and social awareness. When you volunteer, you step outside your own bubble and into the shoes of others, building empathy and understanding as naturally as breathing. You learn to see the world through different lenses, each offering a unique perspective. This journey not only enriches your own life but also fosters a sense of belonging and purpose. Leadership and teamwork skills blossom as you collaborate with others, whether it's organizing a charity event or simply lending a hand at a local food bank. These experiences teach you to work with diverse groups, harnessing the power of unity and cooperation.

Finding volunteer opportunities might seem daunting at first, like searching for a needle in a haystack. But fear not! Start by researching local charities and non-profits that align with your interests.

Are you passionate about animals? Consider volunteering at a local shelter. Love books? Libraries often have programs seeking help. Participating in community service projects is another great way to get involved. Whether it's a neighborhood cleanup or a fundraising event, these projects not only benefit the community but also provide a platform for you to apply and develop your skills. Reach out to schools, religious organizations, or community centers to discover projects that need an extra pair of hands.

The impact of volunteering extends beyond the warm fuzzies it gives you. It's like a secret weapon for your resume, showcasing transferable skills that are highly sought after by employers. Problem-solving, communication and adaptability are just a few of the skills you can highlight, demonstrating your ability to thrive in various situations. Volunteering also provides excellent networking opportunities. You never know who you'll meet while painting murals or serving meals. These connections can lead to job referrals, mentorship and even friendships that last a lifetime.

It's a chance to expand your professional circle with individuals who share your passion for making a difference.

Reflecting on your volunteer experiences is crucial for personal development, offering insights that help you grow. Keeping a *volunteer journal* allows you to document your experiences, challenges and triumphs. By writing down what you've learned, you create a record of your journey and the impact you've made. Sharing volunteer stories with peers can also be incredibly rewarding. It's like swapping tales around a campfire, each story sparking inspiration and encouraging others to get involved. These reflections can reveal new strengths and passions, guiding you toward future opportunities and helping you understand the value of your contributions.

Community involvement is not just about giving back, it's about enriching your own life, too. Through volunteering, you gain a deeper understanding of the world and your place within it. You become part of something bigger, a force for good that helps shape a brighter future. As you reflect on your experiences, you'll find that the skills and connections you've gained are as valuable as the good you've done. Volunteering is a powerful tool for personal growth and career enhancement, offering a path toward a more fulfilling life.

CONCLUSION

Wow, what a journey we've been on together! We've covered so much ground, from the nitty-gritty of budgeting and digital literacy to the big questions of self-discovery and career planning. It's like we've climbed a mountain of knowledge and now we're standing at the summit, enjoying the breathtaking view of all we've accomplished.

Let's take a quick trip down memory lane, shall we? We started off by diving into the world of financial literacy, learning how to make our money work for us instead of the other way around. We tackled budgeting, saving, credit and even dipped our toes into the exciting world of investing. Hopefully, we've become our own personal finance gurus!

Next, we explored the realm of emotional intelligence, learning how to navigate our feelings like a pro. We discovered techniques for managing stress, building resilience and practicing mindfulness. Understanding emotional intelligence will help us deal with life's ups and downs like superheroes.

But we didn't stop there. We also got practical, mastering essential life skills like cooking, car maintenance and even navigating public transportation. We learned how to create a space that inspires us and how to take care of ourselves inside and out. It's like we've become real-life adulting experts!

Of course, we couldn't forget about the digital world. We learned how to stay safe online, communicate effectively and even build a standout resume. We've become tech-savvy wizards, ready to conquer the digital landscape.

And let's not forget about the big picture. We explored our passions, discovered our strengths and started thinking about our future careers. We learned the importance of networking, continuous learning and giving back to our communities. So now we should be equipped to easily become architects of our own destiny!

But here's the thing, this book isn't just a collection of tips and tricks. It's a roadmap for navigating the twists and turns of life with confidence and resilience. It's a reminder that you have the power, ability and skills to shape your own future, no matter what challenges come your way.

So what now? It's time to take all that you've learned and put it into action!

Set some goals for yourself, whether it's starting a budget, practicing mindfulness, or exploring a new career path. And remember, growth doesn't happen overnight. It's a continuous journey of learning and self-discovery.

But remember, you're not alone on this journey. You have a lot of support from your network, family, friends and all the incredible people in your life. They want you to succeed and will support you every step of the way. Don't be afraid to reach out for help when you need it, whether it's to a trusted friend, a mentor, or a professional.

And most importantly, keep learning and growing! The world is full of opportunities for discovery and adventure. Embrace new experiences, challenge yourself and never stop asking questions. You never know what amazing things you might uncover.

I want to thank you from the bottom of my heart for embarking on this journey with me. Your dedication and enthusiasm have been truly inspiring. I hope this book has given you the tools and confidence you need to tackle whatever life throws your way.

But don't just take my word for it. I want to hear from you! Share your experiences, your triumphs and even your struggles. Your story has the power to inspire and encourage others.

So go out there and make your mark on the world! Remember, you have the power to create a life that is uniquely and wonderfully yours. Embrace your quirks, celebrate your strengths and never stop striving for greatness.

I'll be cheering you on every step of the way. Here's to a future filled with endless possibilities and a life lived to the fullest!

With gratitude and support,

   - Freedom Publications: 'Your Partner in Personal Growth and Success'

REFERENCES

Budgeting Tips for Teens in 6 Easy Steps (n.d.) - Better Money Habits
https://bettermoneyhabits.bankofamerica.com/en/personal-banking/teaching-children-how-to-budget

GoHenry. (2024, January 10). *The 8 best budgeting & money apps for kids & teens: 2024 guide Hohenry.com;* GoHenry
https://www.gohenry.com/uk/blog/financial-education/the-best-budgeting-apps-for-families

Ludin, G. (2024, December 24). *Emergency Funds 101: Why Every Young Adult Needs One (And How to Start).* Step.com.
https://step.com/money-101/post/emergency-funds-101-why-every-young-adult-needs-one-and-how-to-start

Warren, K. (2023, March 3). *Credit Tips for Teens.* Investopedia.
https://www.investopedia.com/credit-tips-for-teens-7152864

The Cost of Borrowing & Inflation | Sapling. (n.d.)
https://www.sapling.com/the-cost-of-borrowing--inflation.html

The Best Financial Advice for Young Adults - Car Rental In Prague.
https://www.carrentalinprague.com/the-best-financial-advice-for-young-adults/

The Best Way to Invest Money: 5 Simple Strategies to Start Investing Your Money Today - The Riddle Review. (2023, June 23).
http://www.pc-mobile.net/what-is-the-best-way-to-invest-money/

The Beginner's Guide to Stock Market Investing - Slope. (2023, July 26).
https://slope-wcopilot.webflow.io/resources/the-beginners-guide-to-stock-market-investing

Getting the Most Value for Your Money: Finding the Best Products | Fresh Milk FL.
https://freshmilkfl.com/25078-getting-the-most-value-for-your-money-finding-the-best-products-07/

Weinstein, T. (2024, January 3). *How to Help Teens Build Emotional Intelligence.* Newport Academy
https://www.newportacademy.com/resources/empowering-teens/teen-emotional-intelligence/

REFERENCES

Stress Management and Teens. (2019, January). American Academy of Child and Adolescent Psychiatry; The American Academy of Child and Adolescent Psychiatry.
https://www.aacap.org/AACAP/Families_and_Youth/Facts_for_Families/FFF-Guide/Helping-Teenagers-With-Stress-066.aspx

Building resilience in adolescents and young adults. (2024). UK HealthCare
https://ukhealthcare.uky.edu/wellness-community/blog/building-resilience-adolescents-and-young-adults

Reshyl Del Pilar: 7 Practical Strategies to Overcome Sadness and Reignite Your Joy. (2024 July 19).
http://www.reshyldelpilar.com/2024/07/7-practical-strategies-to-over come.html

Tang, D.-F., Mo, L.-Q., Zhou, X.-C., Shu, J.-H., Wu, L., Wang, D., & Dai, F. (2021). *Effects of mindfulness-based intervention on adolescents emotional disorders: A protocol for systematic review and meta-analysis.* Medicine, 100 (51), e28295
https://pmc.ncbi.nlm.nih.gov/articles/PMC8701759/

Twenty kitchen skills every teen needs to know before they leave for University. (2022, May 26). The Organic Cookery School.
https://www.organiccookeryschool.org/blog//20-kitchen-skills-every-teen-needs-to-know-before-they-leave-for-uni

Essential Car-Care Tips for First-Time Owners (2024 May 16) Consumer Reports.
https://www.consumerreports.org/cars/car-repair-maintenance/car-care-basics-for-first-time-owners-a4141980086/

Home Repair 101: Basic DIY Skills to Teach Your Teens (2024, August 16). C & C Farm & Home.
https://candcfarmandhome.com/home-repair-101-basic-diy-skills-to-teach-your-teens/

Hygiene Basics (for Teens)- KidsHealth. (2019) Kidshealth.org.
https://kidshealth.org/en/teens/hygiene-basics.html

Steps You Should Take if Your Credit Card Gets Hacked. (2014, May 19).
https://www.techcareers.com/articles/Steps-You-Should-Take-if-Your-Credit-Card-Gets-Hacked-14805-article.html

Post Now, Regret Later: The Effects of Your Digital Footprint on College Admissions. (2019, November 13). Kis.ac.th.
https://www.kis.ac.th/connect/news-events/news-template/~board/kis-news/post/post-now-regret-later-the-effects-of-your-digital-footprint-on-college-admissions

Chavez, K. (2023, November 16). *Tools to Protect Your Privacy on Social Media.* NetChoice.
https://netchoice.org/tools-to-protect-your-privacy-on-social-media/

About Us - Bloger Go.
https://blogergo.com/about-us/

Espelage, D. L., & Hong, J. S. (2016).Cyberbullying Prevention and Intervention Efforts: Current Knowledge and Future Directions. *The Canadian Journal of Psychiatry*, 62(6), 374-380
https://pmc.ncbi.nlm.nih.gov/articles/PMC5455869/

Mayo Clinic Staff. (2024, January 18). *Teens and social media use: What's the impact?* Mayo Clinic; Mayo Foundation for Medical Education and Research
https://www.mayoclinic.org/healthy-lifestyle/tween-and-teen-health/in-depth/teens-and-social-media-use/art-20474437

O'Bryan, A. (2022). *How to Practice Active Listening: 16 Examples & Techniques.* Positive Psychology.
https://positivepsychology.com/active-listening-techniques/

Wong, D. (2024, April 8).*Communication Skills for Teens: 7 Skills Every Teen Should Develop - Daniel Wong.* Daniel Wong.
https://www.daniel-wong.com/2024/04/08/communication-skills-for-teens/

Conflict Resolution Strategies - How to Resolve a Conflict in 7 Simple Steps. (2017, May 26). Paradigm Treatment.
https://paradigmtreatment.com/resolve-a-conflict-7-simple-steps/

Jackson, L. (2022, September 6). *Building Trust with Teenagers.* The Gottman Institute.
https://www.gottman.com/blog/building-trust-with-teenagers/

Cappetta, K. (2023, August 22). *Help Teens Learn Time Management Skills | Connections Academy®.* Www.connectionsacademy.com.
https://www.connectionsacademy.com/support/resources/article/time-management-for-teens/

Gupta, S. (2022, December 19). *What Is the Pomodoro Technique?* Verywell Mind.
https://www.verywellmind.com/pomodoro-technique-history-steps-benefits-and-drawbacks-6892111

Effective Time Management Tools for Teens with ADHD - Serenity Wellness. (2024, October 14). Serenity Wellness.
https://serenitywellnessandcounseling.com/effective-time-management-tools-for-teens-with-adhd/#:

biglifejournal.com. (2020). *How to Help Teens Set Effective Goals (Tips & Templates).* Big Life Journal.
https://biglifejournal.com/blogs/blog/guide-effective-goal-setting-teens-template-worksheet?

REFERENCES

Schools Info. (2024, January 29). *The Importance of Identifying Hidden Talents in Children*. Medium.
https://cbseschoolspatiala.medium.com/the-importance-of-identifying-hidden-talents-in-children-599305a01016

The 4 R's of Successful Test Takers.
https://www.crosswalkeducation.com/post/the-4-r-s-of-successful-test-takers-1

Turk, H., & Turk, H. (2023, January 27). *Activity for Teens: Identifying Core Values - Just Be U - Teen/Elementary Curriculum for Girls - a Life-Changing Curriculum for Any Girl*.
https://justbeu.com/identifying-core-values-teens/

Ginsburg, K. (2018, September 4). *Effective strategies to boost teen confidence*. Center for Parent and Teen Communication.
https://parentandteen.com/raising-teens-with-confidence-one-of-the-7-cs-of-resilience/

supportleadrevenue. (2022, October 19). *8 Reasons Why Your Car Sounds Like A Helicopter (When It Shouldn't!) - Glendale Nissan*.
https://www.glendalenissanla.com/2022/10/19/8-reasons-why-your-car-sounds-like-a-helicopter-when-it-shouldnt/

Ordonez, L. (2023, October 8). *How to Help Your Teen Create a Vision Board – HOUSE OF HOPE*. HOUSE of HOPE.
https://nationalhouseofhope.org/2023/how-to-help-your-teen-create-a-vision-board/

McCallister, M. (2024, October). *The Importance of Early Career Exposure for Kids (and How Scouting Helps) - Laurel Highlands Council*. Laurel Highlands Council.
https://lhcscouting.org/the-importance-of-early-career-exposure-for-kids-and-how-scouting-helps/#:

Teen Resume Examples, Templates & Expert Tips. (2024, October 16). MyPerfectResume.
https://www.myperfectresume.com/career-center/resumes/how-to/teens

Team, T. F. (2020, September 21). *Foundations Asheville*. Foundations Asheville.
https://foundationsasheville.com/tips-for-young-adults-going-on-their-first-job-interview/

Networking Basics for High School Students – BigFuture. (n.d.). Bigfuture.collegeboard.org.
https://bigfuture.collegeboard.org/explore-careers/get-started/career-prep-high-school/networking-basics-for-high-school-students

Strategies for Success: How To Monitor & Adjust Your Fitness Journey. (2024, January 22)
https://www.blenderbottle.com/blogs/health/strategies-for-success-how-to-monitor-adjust-your-fitness-journey

10 Easy Stress Relief Exercises You Can Do at Your Desk or Anywhere - Sports Wholesale Supply. (2020, March 30) https://www.sportswholesalesupply.com/blogs/sws-blog/10-easy-stress-relief-exercises-you-can-do-at-your-desk-or-anywhere

Faith and Resilience: How Religion Guides Individuals through Life's Challenges – Info Net Insider. (2024 January 12). https://infonetinsider.com/faith-and-resilience-how-religion-guides-individuals-through-lifes-challenges/

How to Develop Resilience in the Face of Chronic Illness? - Thunderbailbonds. (2024, February 4) https://thunderbailbonds.com/archives/250

ABOUT THE PUBLISHER

Freedom Publications is a respected name, dedicated to providing readers from all walks of life with the tools and insights to succeed in today's competitive and ever-evolving world. Our books cater to teams, leaders, managers, entrepreneurs, professionals, executives, parents, teens, caregivers, educators and everyday individuals eager to sharpen their skills, elevate their thinking and make impactful changes in their careers and lives.

Our books are carefully crafted to deliver practical, accessible guidance on everything from building cohesive teams and inspiring effective leadership to boosting productivity and achieving personal and professional goals. With a focus on real-world applications, our books empower readers to turn concepts into actionable strategies that benefit both individuals and groups, enabling stronger communication, smarter decision-making and sustained success across any field.

Whether you're a business leader striving to lead your team with vision, a professional looking to grow your skill set, an entrepreneur ready to take your venture to the next level, or simply someone interested in improving everyday effectiveness, Freedom Publications is your essential resource for the insights and knowledge to thrive in every aspect of modern business.

- **Freedom Publications: 'Your Partner in Personal Growth and Success'**

If you enjoyed this book and found it helpful, we'd appreciate it if you left a favourable review on Amazon.

www.ingramcontent.com/pod-product-compliance
Lightning Source LLC
Chambersburg PA
CBHW050435010526
44118CB00013B/1534